Your Towns and Cities in th

Whitehaven
in the Great War

Your Towns and Cities in the Great War

Whitehaven
in the Great War

Ruth Mansergh

Pen & Sword
MILITARY

First published in Great Britain in 2015 by
PEN & SWORD MILITARY
an imprint of
Pen and Sword Books Ltd
47 Church Street
Barnsley
South Yorkshire S70 2AS

ISBN 978 1 47383 399 9

Printed and bound in England
by CPI Group (UK) Ltd, Croydon, CR0 4YY

Typeset in Times New Roman

Pen & Sword Books Ltd incorporates the imprints of
Pen & Sword Archaeology, Atlas, Aviation, Battleground, Discovery,
Family History, History, Maritime, Military, Naval, Politics, Railways,
Select, Social History, Transport, True Crime, and Claymore Press,
Frontline Books, Leo Cooper, Praetorian Press, Remember When,
Seaforth Publishing and Wharncliffe.
For a complete list of Pen and Sword titles please contact
Pen and Sword Books Limited
47 Church Street, Barnsley, South Yorkshire, S70 2AS, England
E-mail: enquiries@pen-and-sword.co.uk
Website: **www.pen-and-sword.co.uk**

Contents

The Author

I AM A mother-of-two who has worked as a journalist and as a freelance sub-editor/proofreader. My degree was in English with Social History because of my interest in the history of the north of England. I maintain a positive approach to life despite a disability that has led to several set-backs. I was educated at Harecroft Hall, a prep school near Gosforth south of Whitehaven, Giggleswick and Leeds University.

Thanks to my partner Alan McClenaghan for his computer wizardry with Photoshop and help with setting up a promotional website. I am also grateful to local historians for their generosity with their research and photos that have been collected over many years, with very special thanks going to Ian Stuart Nicholson for his invaluable help.

I have made every effort to contact copyright holders where appropriate and will be happy to update any omissions in any future edition of this book.

Introduction

THIS BOOK IS about Whitehaven's contribution to the Great War effort. 625 Whitehaven men lost their lives in a Cumberland mining town that in 1901 had a population of 21,523. Research about the surrounding area is largely confined to Copeland, between Distington and the Duddon Valley.

War memorials to those killed in the First World War have been moved following church closures; this book also acts as a reference guide to where these memorials are now.

I have gone to great effort to cross-check information with dedicated local historians. While historical documents contain valuable information, inaccuracies also appear. And, as research continues, the number of people who are known to have died during First World War is also rising. For those who are moved to do more research, the *Whitehaven News* is an invaluable resource and contains a great deal of information which I was unable to include here by reason of space.

Cumberland and Westmorland, the Furness area of Lancashire and a

Whitehaven Harbour from Grand Hotel, 1908. In 1998, the town was awarded a lottery grant for regeneration of the harbour area

small bit of Yorkshire became part of Cumbria with the national boundary changes in 1974. Whitehaven, or Whitehebben in Cumbrian chat, is equidistant between Carlisle and Barrow-in-Furness, a large industrial town. The main towns neighbouring Whitehaven, in the borough of Copeland, are Workington and Maryport to the north, Cleator Moor to the east and Egremont to the south. St Bees, a seaside village with a public school Leefe Robinson attended, is four miles south of Whitehaven and Seascale is 15 miles south of Whitehaven. Millom, also in Copeland, is 30 miles south of Whitehaven and is where 1,000 Belgian refugees stayed during the First World War.

The Priory of St Bees owned the village of Whitehaven – a fishing village until the seventeenth century - until Henry VIII dissolved the monasteries in 1539. In 1630, Sir Christopher Lowther used Whitehaven to export coal, chiefly to Dublin and other Irish ports.

In the eighteenth century, tobacco brought home from Virginia to Whitehaven was shipped out again, as it was chiefly a re-export or entrepot trade. Some was absorbed into local manufacture, for example a 'snuffery' in 1733. Whitehaven's last contribution to the tobacco trade was made by the firm of George Jackson & Co, Tangier Street, who marketed various 'cuts' of tobacco and cigarettes under the brand name of Sea Dog. The tobacco they used was not imported directly. Production appears to have terminated around the end of the First World War.

Whitehaven had been a leading rum port since the late seventeenth century and in the winter of 1914, the rum ration was initially given to soldiers to combat the chill and damp of the trenches. Army officer Captain Alexander Stewart said: 'The finest thing that ever happened in the trenches was the rum ration, and never was it more needed than on the Somme.' Meanwhile, from October 1915 onwards, it was illegal in Britain to treat other people to a round of drinks. Too much alcohol was thought to be damaging to productivity!

More than seventy pits were sunk in the Whitehaven and district area in 300 years, and accidents and explosions claimed many lives. The Wellington Pit disaster, on 11 May 1910, remains Cumbria's worst mining accident. A number of First World War soldiers had a mining background. Private Alfred Thompson, who died on 5 June 1916 aged 20 and is on the Lonsdale Roll of Honour, was formerly a coke worker at the William Pit mine. He, the son of James and Catherine Thompson of Stainburn, Workington, was killed coming back from the trench raid of 5 June 1916, carrying a wounded corporal back to British Lines. He is buried at Authuille Military Cemetery, Somme.

Robert Houston Crosby (1896-1939), Border Regiment, of Peter Street, Whitehaven won the Military Medal twice during the war. He was a miner at William Pit and also the recipient of a gold watch from the Coal Conciliation Board 'for conspicuous bravery in the field, France 1917'. In 1915, he suffered a head wound but kept his life when a bullet was deflected by his cap badge. He had been gassed three times and also had an operation to save his leg carried out by an American medical officer. He was given anti-tetanus treatment at a time when tetanus was a key cause of death for the wounded soldiers of the First World War.

After joining the Border Regiment in April 1915, Peter Chambers (died 1954) of Peter Street, Whitehaven was transferred three months later to the Royal Engineers age 35 and to 176th Tunnelling Company. Here he was required to use his mining skills. He won the Military Medal and a gold watch from the Coal Conciliation Board for gallant and conspicuous service in France, November 1918. After the war, Chambers returned to civvy street and became a coal trimmer, levelling out the loads on the coal boats that came into Whitehaven harbour.

Nicknamed the Moles, the tunnelling companies were specialist units of the Corps of Royal Engineers formed to dig attacking tunnels under enemy lines during the First World War. They were a highly respected breed due to the harsh conditions they endured. They dug under the trenches in France, into the German lines. The last Whitehaven pit, Haig, ceased mining on 31 March 1986.

Whitehaven was also a shipbuilding town and the largest ship built there, the *Alice A. Leigh* ran into trouble during the First World War. She was nearly sunk by a German submarine, *U-32,* in 1916 in the Mediterranean. Ordered to disembark, crew and passengers were rowing away from the Alice when the French destroyer Gabion sped to the scene. *U-32* escaped but the ship was saved. On another occasion, the *Alice* had to sail through the centre of a typhoon. This demasted the barque. She was sold in 1917 to New York & Pacific Steam Ship Company.

Perhaps because of its rural situation, a good proportion of the population of Cumberland had a less arduous time with regard to food rationing in the First World War than most city dwellers. But unrest and riots broke out in west Cumbria in early 1917 when the price of potatoes saw a fourfold increase. In the Maryport Christmas market, a boycott by housewives reduced geese from one and thruppence to nine pence per pound, a 60 per cent reduction, and the women were ultimately as successful with potatoes as with geese. In January 1917, they sent the town crier around to make sure that everybody was united and asked women not to buy – to boycott the cost of potatoes at a ridiculously high price. There was some difficulty; some of the farmers decided they were just going to take their crops home. Others did give in and sold for a shilling to clear their stocks and off they went back home. But carts were overturned, people were hurt and generally the story spread through the rest of the county. There were disturbances and riots the following week in Carlisle market. In Keswick, there was 'a bit of a do' with two farmers who turned up wanting to market one day, and some soldiers got involved on the side of the housewives; the carts were overturned and the boys in the town were suddenly seen with their caps and their pockets bulging with potatoes as they scurried around trying to pick them up as they fell off.

The other fall-out from this was the theft of potatoes. Marian Atkinson, aged 97 in 2003, spoke to oral historians Richard van Emden and Steve Humphries. She grew up in the Lake District and was a 12-year-old schoolgirl in 1917: 'We'd see turnips, potatoes and cabbage and we'd decide what we'd pinch on the way home. On the way back, the bigger boys used to say "Keep your eyes rolling for the farmer".' My parents wouldn't accept anything stolen – they used to make us take it back – so we used to sit under a hedge and gnaw the vegetables like a rabbit. If we could hear the farmers' horses clip-clopping, we used to bung what we'd been eating under the hedge and go like lightning back home, large as life.'

In February 1918, there was a serious accident at Cleator Moor when a woman was trampled in a butcher's queue (*Whitehaven News* 7 February 1918). The national meat rationing scheme started on 25 March 1918. In April 1918, Whitehaven Borough urged householders to keep pigs. And a Soup Kitchen opened in Whitehaven on 13 November 1918.

And finally there was peace – Tuesday 12 November 1918, a day after the signing of the Armistice, dawned a fine bright day. Never in Whitehaven was there so great a gathering as for the Thanksgiving Service at 3pm, which began with a procession of the Mayor and Corporation from the Town Hall. The service was attended by the Clergy of all the denominations in the town. The Sermon was preached by the Congregational Minister H Stowell who had been a War Chaplain. The collection was taken for the Church Army and the YMCA – the latter in particular having played such a fine role in supporting the troops throughout the conflict. The children had been due to start back to school on Tuesday 19 November. Instead, they found themselves in a

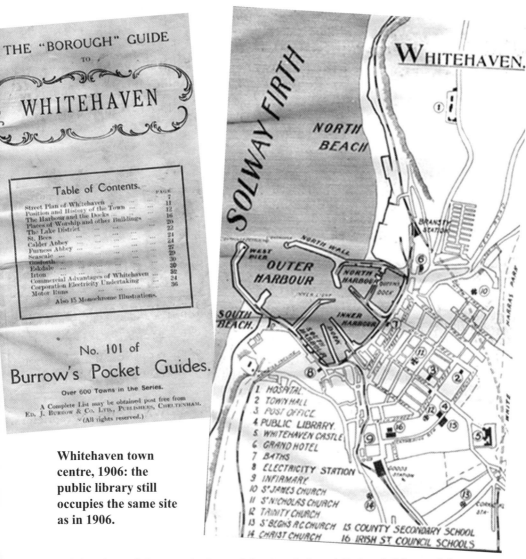

THE "BOROUGH" GUIDE
TO
WHITEHAVEN

Table of Contents.

No. 101 of
Burrow's Pocket Guides.

Over 600 Towns in the Series.

A Complete List may be obtained post free from
ED. J. BURROW & CO. LTD., PUBLISHERS, CHELTENHAM.
(All rights reserved.)

Whitehaven town centre, 1906: the public library still occupies the same site as in 1906.

SOLWAY FIRTH

WHITEHAVEN.

NORTH BEACH

BRANSTY STATION

WEST PIER

NORTH WALL

OUTER HARBOUR

NORTH HARBOUR

QUEENS DOCK

SOUTH BEACH.

INNER HARBOUR

MARASI PARK

1 HOSPITAL
2 TOWN HALL
3 POST OFFICE
4 PUBLIC LIBRARY
5 WHITEHAVEN CASTLE
6 GRAND HOTEL
7 BATHS
8 ELECTRICITY STATION
9 INFIRMARY
10 ST JAMES CHURCH
11 ST NICHOLAS CHURCH
12 TRINITY CHURCH
13 ST BEGHS RC CHURCH
14 CHRIST CHURCH
15 COUNTY SECONDARY SCHOOL
16 IRISH ST COUNCIL SCHOOLS

celebration of the conclusion of the Armistice. All the children of the town were given a Peace Medal on Armistice Day 1919. The only other place in Cumbria to have such medals was Carlisle.

Chapter One

Recruits needed

IN 1899, IRISH volunteers for the Second Anglo-Boer War (1899-1902) landed at Maryport and marched through the district to embark at Whitehaven docks for South Africa. After the relief of Mafeking on 16/17 May 1900, villagers at Moresby, Whitehaven, joined in the celebrations when miners dragged sleepers and tar from the pit and built a bonfire that could be seen for miles. At Seascale, the celebration took the form of a procession; each child was presented with sweets, chocolate and a small flag. By 4 August 1914, Britain was again at war, this time 'the war to end all wars'.

German commanders tended to think that Britain's entry into the war would make little difference. Britannia certainly ruled the waves with the world's largest navy, but as the Kaiser said disparagingly to his generals: 'Dreadnoughts have no wheels'. Unlike Britain, all the continental powers had huge armies, enrolled or formed by conscription. In 1914, the British army consisted of just over 730,000 officers and men. One-third of them served in the regular army itself, with the greater part stationed in reserve formations, the most notable of which was the Territorial Force (TF; it subsequently became the Territorial Army). The TF was envisaged as a home defence force for service during wartime.

The Border Regiment (1881-1959), based in Carlisle and named after England's border with Scotland, was only five battalions in strength – two regular, one reserve (3rd) and two TF – on the outbreak of the First World War. The 2nd Battalion (regular) was mobilised for war on 6 October 1914. In its first encounter with the enemy at Kruiseik Hill, Belgium, the men of the 2nd Battalion were surrounded in their trenches on three sides by the enemy.

As the conflict progressed, the Border Regiment expanded to form sixteen battalions. Six of the regiment's battalions took part in the Battle of the Somme (1 July to 18 November on both sides of the River Somme), one of the bloodiest battles in human history. Other battle honours

Cap Badge of the Border Regiment.

Border Regiment off to the War.

include Langemarck, Belgium 1914-17 where the Germans first used poison gas on 22 April 1915.

With conscription politically unpalatable, Lord Kitchener, the newly-appointed Secretary of State for War, decided to raise a new army of volunteers. Men were invited to volunteer with their friends, family and colleagues to form the Pals Battalions.

The 11th (Service) Battalion Border Regiment (Lonsdale) – comprising local men drawn from the railways, factories, shops and fields of Cumberland and Westmorland – was one of the Pals Battalions and it was formed in September 1914. Lord Lonsdale – the Yellow Earl, who had a residence at Whitehaven Castle (never a castle in the true sense of the word) – took a great deal of pride in the battalion named after him and paid for their equipment with his own money, issuing the men with a solid silver hallmarked cap badge that he commissioned. He planned 'his' uniform to be of hodden grey 'manufactured in the Cumberland Mills', perhaps forgetting that the Germans had already taken up that option, but the army overruled him, saying it had to be khaki.

Recruiting offices in Kendal, Workington and Carlisle had raised 642 men for the battalion by the end of October 1914. The drawback of Pals

Battalions was that a whole town could lose its military-aged menfolk in a single day. When Lord Lonsdale was recruiting men for his Lonsdale Battalion, the Mayor of Whitehaven, Herbert Wilson Walker (1875-1934), travelled through to Lowther Castle, the family seat of the Earls of Lonsdale, asking Lord Lonsdale to stop recruiting as it was going to affect coal production. Lord Lonsdale said he was too busy to see Mr Walker, who was mayor between 1913 and 1915, who then had to travel back home.

Lonsdale cap badge: It featured the family crest of a griffin. Apart from the cap badge, the Lonsdale uniform was identical to every other soldier's uniform.

Make do and mend: Soldiers training on Blackwell Racecourse, Carlisle in March 1916. The soldiers even lacked basic equipment such as a rifle and a uniform until 1915.

There wasn't any 'local' training. The Lonsdales trained on Blackwell Racecourse on the edge of Carlisle. Initially, conditions at Blackwell Racecourse were so inadequate that soldiers who could return would go back home to sleep at night. Those who could not made themselves as comfortable as they could in the empty horse boxes and the grandstand; eventually, wooden huts were erected.

In November 1914, St George's Theatre, Kendal showed all week a special local picture secured at Blackwell, 'A Day with the Lonsdale Battalion'; scenes included physical and company drill, full parade, dinner time, preparing meals and Lord Lonsdale in Camp. The Lonsdales did a lot of trench digging there. By March 1915, the battalion had swelled to 1,350 and on 8 May they left Blackwell for the final stages of training on Salisbury Plain.

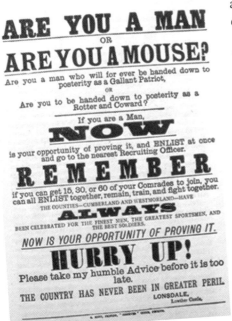

Are You a Man or a Mouse: The recruiting poster that Lonsdale had printed, said to be a slur on manhood, caused quite a storm.

On the opening day of the Battle of the Somme on 1 July 1916, the Lonsdales suffered more than 500 casualties out of the 800 who went into action. The commanding officer of the Lonsdales, Lieutenant-Colonel Percy Wilfred Machell (1862-1916), age 52, of Crackenthorpe Hall, Westmorland was killed on 1 July.

Some of the lads from the Irish community in West Cumberland enlisted with the Tyneside Irish (Northumberland Fusiliers) Pals Battalion. This brigade initially trained over in Northumberland, many in the Alnwick area.

Machell is also commemorated on Appleby St Lawrence Church Memorial. He was married in 1905 to Valda, Countess of Gleichen, a singer.

16

Chapter Two

Prove your skill; try and reach the Cumberland coast

SEASCALE HAD A muzzle loading cannon (1909-1940) located on the foreshore as a tourist attraction. It was fixed by the Furness Railway. The *Whitehaven News* of February 1910 reported:

'The inhabitants of Seascale who have had their mind much agitated and alarmed as of late by the so-called German scare will have been made easy that no invasion is possible, now that a large cannon has just been fixed behind the waiting room of Seascale station, overlooking the sea.'

But it would seem that the Germans were unimpressed by the Seascale cannon (which was melted down in 1940 as part of the war effort), and perhaps by the Braystones cannon.

The Germans' most formidable naval weapon was the U-boat, a submarine far more sophisticated than those built by other nations at the time. On Monday 16 August 1915, *U-24* surfaced at 4.50am off Parton Bay and proceeded to shell the village of Lowca, a hive of heavy industry largely based upon coal extraction and iron production. Commander Kapitanleutnant Rudolf Schneider's target was the 'top secret' Harrington Coke works that was attached to No 10 Lowca Colliery. The plant had been established by German-controlled firm Koppers, and the works and the potential use of synthetic toluene out of benzene was well known to the Germans.

The Lowca plant was targeted because it manufactured synthetic toluene out of benzene, used to make explosives. A total of 55 shells out of *U-24*'s magazine of 300 were aimed at the works in 55 minutes. But for such a daring effort, the rewards were small:

Schneider (1881-1917) had already sunk HMS *Formidable* during the very first underwater attack at night on 1 January 1915 off Portland Bill, Dorset.

Parton, looking north, with Lowca Colliery in the distance.
Cumbrian Railways Association

30 hits were recorded on the works, but only four did any damage. A 50-gallon drum of Benzol was set ablaze, which spread to the loading tanks, and there were holes in two 11,000-gallon Naphtha tanks, which did not ignite. The powerhouse had also been hit with a 'Dud' shell and its chimney was left with a hole in it. 900 windows were also broken and another shell landed in the garden of a house at Howgate.

However, the works' owners had a well-rehearsed wartime plan in force: if it came under attack from Zeppelins or warships, certain valves and steam traps were to be fully opened, and six blasts given on the steam whistle, warning the villagers to flee. The engineer on duty, Oscar Ohlson, along with his valve-man Dan Thompson, released flaming gas into the atmosphere, which produced a great cloud of smoke – this seems to have convinced the Germans a vital target had been hit. The U-boat then submerged.

No-one was injured, apart from a dog called Lion hit by a stray shell splinter. William Twentyman, stationmaster/goods agent at Parton, about one-and-a-half miles north of Whitehaven, held back a Whitehaven-bound passenger train in his station until the shelling stopped. German warships had already attacked a plant at South Shields which was producing toluene from benzol and severely damaged it, so production at Lowca had already been increased. The report from a Munich paper of the U-boat raid said that, although the military effect of the bombardment of the Cumberland coast was not very considerable, its

Parton Bay: In the 18th century, Parton was a notorious rendezvous for smugglers.

significance as a feature of the Anglo-German naval war was great: 'The extreme importance of this bombardment lies in the fact that it proves that the British fleet is not able even to protect the coasts of the Irish Sea from attack by German warships.'

The best contemporary account of the Lowca raid seems to be a poem by Joseph Holmes (1859-1930) of Siddick, then a stationmaster on the Lowca light railway passenger line (opened in 1913). The poem was sold on handbills for 1 penny with the promise that 'Proceeds of sale will be given to the Soldiers' Tobacco Fund' (letters from the front contained a request for 'something to smoke'):

The Bombardment of the Cumberland Coast

On August Sixteenth, old Kaiser Bill
Said to his men, 'Now prove your skill,
And try and reach the Cumberland coast,
The feat of which I'd like to boast.'

The Kaiser's word they did obey,
And fired away in Parton Bay,
With shot and shell they did their best
To put the Lowca works to rest.

The damage done was not so much,
The Benzol plant they did not touch,
One shell fell here, another there
Which gave the workmen quite a scare.
The inhabitants too grew quite alarmed,

Because this port is still unarmed,
This opportunity the enemy seized,
And rained the shells just where he pleased.

Two shells went through a cottage home,
The father shouts 'A German Bomb,'
The children then ran out like bees,
And joined the Lowca refugees.

The submarine then made its way
Across the dub from Parton Bay,
To find some other defenceless port
Where German fiends could have their sport.

Remember Bill the time will come
When we'll have thee beneath our thumb
And thou wilt wish thou had'st never been born
For we'll treat thee with the utmost scorn.

Thy barbarous deeds and acts are such
We could not punish thee too much.
Don't ask from us to be forgiven
The most fiendish villain under heaven.

Coastal bombardment: Recruitment adverts also capitalised on the 'insulting' attack. *(Whitehaven News)*

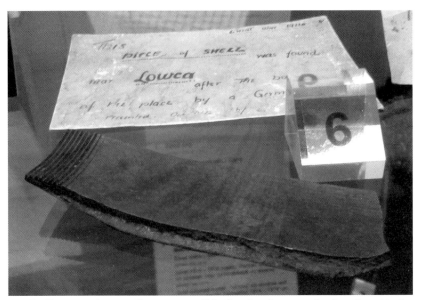

At the Beacon: An artefact responsible for the damage during the attack. The 'nose cone' shell is one of 50 that were fired. *(Taken by author summer 2014)*

Also at the Beacon is a memorial to Lion the Dog. It reads:

Moral of the Bombardment:
We had better take
our coats off
If the Huns we're
going to shift
Supply the wants of
the firing line
is one way of
giving a lift
And remember the
task is a tough one
To oust the Germ-Hun swine
For there'll be no rest nor peace on earth
Til he's pushed back over the Rhine.

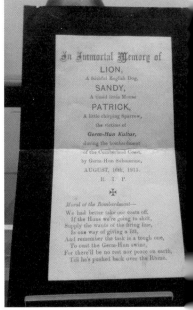

RIP Lion: In memory of Lion the dog, Sandy the mouse, Patrick the sparrow and the victims of Germ-Hun Kultur.
(Taken by author at the Beacon, summer 2014)

Raymond Fitzsimons spoke to *Radio Cumbria* about the Lowca attack in 1984. He said it was the best thing his father had seen since Buffalo Bill came to town. People crowded the pier to get a better view, as to see a U-boat was quite a novelty. Everyone was excited and waved to the German crew and after 50 minutes the U-boat disappeared. It had gone altogether; the town was disappointed. Local people asked why it was there in the first place. They thought that the captain had lost his way and was probably drunk. Whether or not people thought the captain was drunk or lost, the truth is that this was a very deliberate and long diversion.

Jeff Wilson of Distington, author of *Distington the Friendly Parish* (2000), spoke to the BBC in 2014 about the U-boat attack:

> 'Like all good stories, it starts off very simple. Two men out fishing, Captain Cowley and it's understood, Mr Moore. Each had their boat out, probably three-quarters-of-a-mile out from the shore. And they were what Cumbrians call cod banging. Both were within hailing distance of each other and one remarked to the other that he could hear a noise. And at first they thought it was a tar barrel (it was the only object he could comprehend coming up out of the water) that broke the surface and then about 200 tons of machinery emerged from these depths at an angle probably of about 30 degrees. Both men had never seen a submarine before, so here they were confronted by something that was a machine emerging and they wanted to get away.'

Local boys, later on, collected the shrapnel and tried to sell it. Mr Wilson said:

> 'Enterprising that he was, a boy and his friends ran out of shrapnel. They went off to the blacksmiths at the pit and asked him to manufacture more for them. In fact, the gentleman, Mr Holliday, whose house had been drilled by this round, welcomed visitors the next day because thousands had descended on the village to witness this. He put a little saucer outside and you put a penny in and you went in and looked round the house. So I think he recuperated more than he lost.'

He added:

> 'There was no gun of any size that could have opposed this vessel. That caused furore for years afterwards. Should we have mobile guns round here, should they be fixed? In fact during the Second World War, they were fixed; there were massive guns at Workington.'

U-24 was one of three U-boats operating in the Irish Sea around 16 August 1915.

U-27 and *U-38* were off Llandudno as part of a plan to pick up German officers escaping from Aled Duffryn camp, North Wales. *U-24* surrendered to the Allies on 22 November 1918 and was broken up at

Swansea in 1922. And on 13 October 1917, during very stormy weather, Schneider was lost overboard from the conning tower of *U-87*. One of his shipmates managed to bring him back on board but it was too late. He was subsequently buried at sea between the Shetland Isles and Norway.

After the Lowca attack, many local people believed that Hildegarde Burnyeat, the German wife of former Liberal MP and barrister William John Dalzell Burnyeat (1874-1916), had been signalling the U-boat from her nearby home. However, there are conflicting views on whether she was really a spy and the risk she proved. They lived at Moresby House, where they kept a butler, James Brower (age 31 in 1911) from Yorkshire, a cook, Annie Marshall, 27, from Parton and a housemaid, Florence Wright, 25, from Lowca.

Hildegarde, the daughter of a Prussian army officer, remained pro-German throughout the war and her neighbours knew her to be a strong supporter of her homeland and that many of her relatives were fighting against the British. Her brother was serving in the German army and she publicly defended the German methods of warfare.

In the wake of the U-boat raid, she was arrested by the authorities under the Defence of the Realm Act 1914 and interned at Aylesbury Prison, Buckinghamshire. She was still there when her husband died a year later, aged 42, though she was allowed out to visit him during his dying hours. After his death, she was released from internment, apparently on health grounds, and allowed to live with an English family

in Harrogate, causing some antagonism in the Yorkshire spa town. Townsfolk called for an explanation from the Home Office. 'Everybody is asking why Harrogate of all places should have been selected as the residence of this German-born woman,' reported the *Daily Dispatch*. 'It is common knowledge that Mrs Burnyeat is the daughter of a Prussian officer.' There was talk of a public meeting being called to air the issue of ex-internees being sent to Harrogate.

Her husband, the son of local JP and ironmaster William Burnyeat and his wife Sarah Frances (nee Dalzell) of Millgrove, Low Moresby, studied law at Oxford and

German spy-mania: Hildegarde Burnyeat of Berlin, born 1875 in Germany. *(Whitehaven News)*

was Whitehaven's MP between 1906 and 1910. Hildegarde (nee Retzlaff), born in 1875, came from Friedenau, Berlin and married William Burnyeat in September 1908 at the Kaiser Wilhelm Memorial Church in Berlin. The couple met while on holiday in Sicily. When the coke ovens at Lowca were being built by Koppers, some girls from Parton married German workers and returned with them to Germany, prior to the First World War.

On his death, William Burnyeat left the bulk of his estate, gross value £13,834, to Hildegarde for life, or until her remarriage, that is as long as she married a British subject – a caveat he included presumably because of the huge controversy caused by her pro-German sympathies. However, the widowed Hildegarde did remarry a Dutchman – Manta Meindert Schim Van der Loeff – at the Hague in February 1921. It is believed he changed his nationality to English just before the marriage so his wife could keep the money. He died two years later.

William was survived by his father and mother, two brothers and two sisters and his family just weren't having it. A long-drawn-out lawsuit ensued that ended up in the House of Lords. Eventually, the Burnyeats won, but most of the money by then would have probably disappeared in legal fees. Family stories have it that afterwards Hildegarde would write begging letters to the Burnyeat family but these would be immediately despatched to the bin.

On 6 February 1918, the British steamer *Westmoreland* was torpedoed by *UB-57* off the north coast of the Isle of Man before being wrecked off Drigg. Her journey from Wellington, New Zealand was via Halifax, Nova Scotia and she was carrying frozen meat for the troops in France. It was reported in the *Whitehaven News* of 7 February 1918:

Yesterday (Wednesday) the signal for the assembly of the Whitehaven Lifeboat crew was heard in the afternoon. It appears that about 3.15pm a telephone message had been received from the coast watch at Seascale stating that a four masted steamer was ashore off Seascale and that the sea was breaking over her. Mr JG Oldfield, secretary to the lifeboat, and the Harbourmaster, Capt Irving had the lifeboat crew summoned, and tug boat got in readiness to take it down to Seascale. The crew assembled and the boat was launched smartly in ten minutes; but in the meantime a further message was received from the Llandudno coast watch that they had news that there was no crew aboard the steamer. Consequently the lifeboat was recalled.

There was more news a week later, as the *Whitehaven News* of 14

February 1918 reported:

A quantity of wreckage has been washed ashore between Drigg and St Bees, the bulk seemingly on the seashore. Mr WM Dalzell, one of the Coastguard men, intimated to the receiver of wrecks at Whitehaven the large quantity of Australian rabbits that were on the shore, and were fit for food if used at once. Mr Dalzell, in receiving consent to deal with them, at once communicated on the telephone with a number of Food Controllers. Several farmers and carters at once got to work. The rabbits were all gathered up, and carted to the railway station, when the stationmaster and his staff despatched them by rail to the following towns – Whitehaven, Maryport, Millom, Barrow, Dalton, Lancaster and Preston. On Friday the beach was covered with rabbits. On Monday very few could be seen on the shore. Thanks to the efforts of Mr Dalzell and his co-workers, a large number were sent to the places mentioned. Great credit is due to the workers for preventing a waste of good food, especially at these critical times when meat is so scarce.

Threat from the skies: There was a very great fear of the Zeppelin as a weapon of war, but this fancy dress entry in a Millom carnival attempted to make humour from it.

UB-57 was mined off the Flanders coast on 14 October 1918 and all 34 hands were lost. *Westmoreland* was sunk by *U-566* in 1942.

While it was said 'no bombing Zeppelin or Gotha aircraft ever attacked our peaceful backwater during hostilities', precautions were taken. In March 1915, the *West Cumberland Times* reported:

'Farmers and occupiers of land are urged by the Food Production Department to see their property is insured against damage by aircraft or bombardment if it exceeds £500.'

In the same month, the Cockermouth Urban District Council warned in an advert in the newspaper of 'Daylight Air Raids', asking the public to listen for siren warnings 'and shelter indoors until all clear'.

Chapter 3

Carrying on essential production

VICKERS IN BARROW-IN-FURNESS was kept very busy during the war. The company's Barrow shipyard built submarines for the Royal Navy, as it still does today, and large quantities of artillery pieces and munitions were also produced. In West Cumberland, iron ore and coal production increased to cope with rising demand in the First World War and there was a shell factory at Workington.

But did war transform pre-war problems of unemployment and short time into ones of excessive overtime and labour shortages? West Cumberland produced the most vital raw materials of the shipbuilding industry, that of iron and steel. A letter of appeal was sent to Thomas Gavan Duffy, Secretary to the Cumberland Iron Ore Miners' and Kindred Trades Association, for miners to increase working hours from eight to ten in order to increase stocks of haematite iron ore. This was reported in the *Whitehaven News* on 13 May 1915. In August 1915, William Brace (1865-1947), who during the First World War held the post of Under-Secretary of State for the Home Department in Lloyd George's Coalition Government, appealed to Egremont iron-ore miners for increased output (*Whitehaven News* 19 August 1915).

In October 1915, miners at Hodbarrow, Millom (which employed 1,094 in 1914, according to Durham Mining Museum) were asked to work Saturday afternoons to increase output of iron ore. They would not consent. More men were engaged at Hodbarrow to boost output. Also at Millom, there was a meeting of Millom Education Committee in 1917 to discuss the shortage of teachers.

In 1914, Harrington Colliery at Lowca near Whitehaven (closed 1968) employed 1,114 (898 below, 216 surface); Walkmill Colliery, Moresby, Whitehaven employed 706; Wellington Colliery, Whitehaven employed 583; William Colliery, Whitehaven employed 1,057; Whitehaven Colliery employed 700; Cleator iron ore mine was not worked; Jacktrees iron ore mine, Cleator Moor employed fifty-seven; Crossfield iron ore mine, Cleator Moor employed fifty; Montreal iron ore mine, Cleator Moor employed 107; Montreal Colliery, Cleator Moor employed 123; Crowgarth iron ore mine employed sixty-seven; Falcon iron ore mine, Egremont was closed; Fletcher iron ore pit, Cleator employed fourteen; Florence iron ore mine, Egremont employed forty-two; Gillfoot Park iron ore mine, Egremont employed 252; Townhead iron ore mine, Egremont employed 149; Ullbank iron ore mine, Egremont employed fifty-seven; Ullcoats iron ore mine, Egremont employed 336; Pallaflat iron ore mine, Bigrigg employed fifty-two and was abandoned the same year; Park House iron ore mine, Bigrigg employed 422; Sir John Walsh iron ore mine, Bigrigg employed 134; and Postlethwaite's Moor Row iron ore mine employed 116.

Thomas Richardson (1868-1928) served as Labour MP for Whitehaven from 1910 to 1918. He said that those who now stood for peace would in the future be recognised as the true friends of the workers, according to the *Aberdare Leader* newspaper 15 August 1914.

The Germans appreciated the strategic significance of tungsten, a metal which is as dense as gold. The German-owned Cumbrian Mining Company took over Carrock Wolfram Mine, Caldbeck Fells (the nearest town is Wigton) which produced vital tungsten, in 1904 until the outbreak of the First World War. To meet the wartime demand for tungsten, the Government funded the revival of the mine, which enjoyed a brief flourishing until 1921. Tungsten has an incredibly high melting point, and is only second in hardness to diamond. These properties made it a vital component in the manufacture of armour plate for ships and machine tools in the munitions industry.

Cleator Flax Mills, adjacent to the river Ehen, was awarded War Office contracts to make khaki and other fabrics for army uniforms. During April 1915, there was a strike by 250 women workers and twenty boys, due to poor working conditions and low pay. Many mills used child labour, advertising for 'large families with children' as well as overseers to instruct them. After the strike, lasting six weeks, the women and children were given a 10 per cent war bonus by the owners, the Ainsworths, for their hard work.

In 1938, Jakob Spreiregen (b1893), who was working in London as an importer of Basque berets from France, bought the Ainsworths' mill in Cleator and the Kangol hat company was started up. The Kangol building is now derelict, since the company ended its association with the town in 2009.

From 2 March 1916, conscription meant that all men between 18 and 41 had to join up. Those who objected had to appeal in public, usually on moral or religious grounds. It was not an easy process. Generally, miners were automatically exempt from joining the army. Their occupation was considered vital to the country and coal was still required to run factories, to power railways, to make weapons, to fuel homes and to run ships, although many miners opted to enlist. The pits around Whitehaven were not controlled by the Government in the war

– they continued in private hands, being leased from Lowthers.

A very large number of farmers and traders appeared in front of military service tribunals for exemption from conscription. Military tribunals were established under the Derby Scheme (October 1915-December 1915) which invited eligible men to 'attest' their willingness to be called up at a time in the future, in the autumn of 1915 and were simply re-configured and given a different brief after conscription was introduced.

Tribunals met locally, with the press usually in attendance. Tribunals included:

Cumberland County Tribunal; Workington Municipal Borough Tribunal; Millom Urban District Tribunal; Whitehaven Rural District Tribunal; Whitehaven Municipal Borough Tribunal; Cockermouth Urban District Tribunal; Arlecdon and Frizington Urban District Council; Egremont Urban District Tribunal; Cleator Moor Urban District Tribunal; Bootle Rural District Tribunal. The Bootle and Millom Tribunals are the only ones in West Cumbria to have been fully recorded. The Minute Book of the Whitehaven Rural District Tribunal survives at Whitehaven Record Office. The tribunal was formally convened by the Rural District Council on 10 February 1916 and met on forty-nine occasions.

The first tribunal appeals were at the lower local government level – Urban District Council, Rural District Council, Municipal Boroughs, etc.

War Office contracts: Cleator Mill Girls, 1915.

If the appellant were not happy with the decision there, he could appeal to the County Tribunal. There was no freedom to appeal beyond that. The National or Central Appeal Tribunal which met in London was reserved for appeals on matters of law and then only with the approval of the County Tribunals.

Most men were given some kind of exemption, usually temporary or conditional on their situation at work or home remaining serious enough to warrant their retention at home. A lot of the farmers and farm hands just kept on and on getting temporary exemptions as there was just no-one to replace them. Occasionally, labour was found from a national pool but invariably that labour was utterly unsatisfactory. The Bootle Rural Tribunal chairman was William Lewthwaite JP (1853-1927) of

Charles Gilfrid Lewthwaite was awarded the Military Cross.

Broadgate, Thwaites, a major local landowner so he knew very well the importance of the farming industry and keeping the home front going. He did also lose a son, Charles Gilfrid Lewthwaite (1884-1917), 2nd North Midland Brigade, Royal Field Artillery, in the conflict.

Examples of men given exemption are as follows: Joiner John Jackson, 41, of Finch Street, Millom was granted a temporary exemption by Millom Urban Tribunal in June 1916. Also in June 1916, the Bootle Rural Tribunal granted a temporary exemption to farmer Miles Crayston, 18, of Monkfoss, Bootle.

The *Whitehaven News* reported the following on 3 August 1916: Mr James Dawson, grocer with a cycle business, age 34 and of Ulpha in the lakeless dale of Dunnerdale, applied for exemption on the grounds that if he had to go his business would have to be closed, and he could not find anyone to take his place. Mr W Britton Jones (a military representative on the Bootle Rural Tribunal) said that temporary exemption had been granted (two months on 26 May 1916), and no attempt had been made to get anyone in his place. Mr Dawson's wife could do all the business except the cycle repairing. Skilled men were urgently needed in the army, and he should be released. Exemption until 30 September 1916 was granted. He was eventually granted full exemption on 13 October 1916 on the basis that he must work on munitions work part-time – presumably at Vickers, Barrow.

Particularly on the Millom Urban District Tribunal, there were clashes from time to time with the other members. In particular at one stage it was questioned why Britton Jones, a relatively young man, was not fighting at the front rather than being on the tribunals sending other men there.

Chapter 4

We will not go to war

A DATABASE OF British First World War conscientious objectors (COs) compiled by Cyril Pearce, a retired lecturer at Leeds University (who has helped me with current research) contains material for more than 17,000 COs. He portrays the objector as one who reflects the views of those around him. Very few COs were from Cumberland and none at all from Whitehaven. There was one for the 'Whitehaven Rural District' but none from the town itself. Was Cumberland exceptionally patriotic? Perhaps many men who elsewhere might have professed their opposition to the war and to conscription did not do so because they were exempt because of employment regarded as war essential. They kept their heads down.

Meanwhile, the following was sent to the editor of the *Whitehaven News* on 6 September 1917 about 'shirkers' escaping military service:

Whitehaven News
6th September 1917
Surface Labour Protest
(To The Editor Of The *Whitehaven News*.)
Sir, — Would you kindly provide me with a small space of your valuable paper to point out a few facts to the misguided members of the West Cumberland Iron Ore Miners' and Kindred Trades' Association, and of which I am a member?

What have we gained by coming on strike? The majority has gained nothing. The 700 labourers who have gone in as miners contain a large number of men of military age, who flocked to the iron ore mines since 1914 in order to escape military service, which is not fair to the working underground labourers and surface labourers, who were employed at the mines previous to the war, and I think the Council of the Union ought to have insisted that these shirkers should have been called up for military service, the same as the Miners' Federation are doing in regard to men of military age who have gone to the coal mines since August, 1914.

What have the surface workers gained after their three weeks' holiday? In the first offer they got the same terms, as regards money, viz., 1s per day on their wage and a guaranteed production bonus of 5s per week in three months' time, viz., November 1st, with permission to apply for another increase of wages on November 1st, if the first offer was satisfactory; but Executive Council denied the members of their right-to-ballot on the above proposals in accordance with rule 16 of the registered rules of the Association. The Ministry of Munitions promptly offered to go to arbitration, which Executive Council also refused, contrary to rule 16, which states: 'Whenever a proposal of concession is made on either side the ballot must be taken, when a majority of the members on strike or locked out through the strike, shall decide as to whether they shall be accepted or not.' Why should the members submit to the control of Duffy, Edmonds & Co.? It is high time that the members had a weeding out spell at the Miners' Hall, Cleator Moor, and elect a Council which will face the members of the different lodges, and give account of their stewardship, and also to submit any proposals (by the employers) to the ballot, in order to see if they will satisfy the majority of the members.

Eventually the Executive was called to London, to meet Winston [Churchill], and whether Doran had a hand in drawing up the final proposals I cannot say, but such proposals to the day workers (which were accepted by the Executive) are worse than original proposals of Mr. John Hunter, who fixed August 1st for the commencement of the raise in wages, and a promise to consider the question again in three months' time, if not 'satisfactory. Now an agreement has been made with Mr. Churchill for the increase of wages to start on August 27th, production bonus of 5s per week (guaranteed) in three months' time, and such agreement to remain in force to the end of 1918, or the end of the war, whichever is the longest.

On the other hand, the Ministry of Munitions has power to bring in imported labour (to the camps) at Frizington, Bigrigg, Egremont, and Millom to work in the iron ore mines at a wage of 13s per day and 3s per day sustenance allowance (vice 'Daily Despatch,' September 1st, 1917). Mr. Duffy and the Council have during this last twelve months passed resolutions not to have these men in the mines, unto such times as all labourers, top and bottom, were put in as miners, but it has come to nought. The men are coming, and the poor surface labourers have to remain on the top and be content with the miserly increase of 1s per day. This is causing very bitter feeling amongst the labourers. —

Thanking you in anticipation, I remain,

A Surface Labourer

But the idea of men coming to the mines after the war began and before conscription was introduced with the intention of avoiding service is hard to prove. The Surface Labourer's comments can be dismissed as sour grapes.

One of eight 'absentees' and 'deserters' reported in the *Whitehaven News* in 1915, 1916 and 1917 (they were not described as COs) is Thomas Park. He had appeared at Whitehaven Magistrates Court and was on remand having failed to report for military service (*Whitehaven News*, 20 September 1917). He was from Mosser, Cockermouth and ended up serving in the Friends' Ambulance Unit (FAU), founded by the Quakers. Members were trained at Jordans, a hamlet in Buckinghamshire. Altogether, it sent more than 1,000 men to France and Belgium, where they worked on ambulance convoys and ambulance trains with the French and British armies.

Chapter Five

Abraham Acton VC, an Orangeman in Whitehaven

THE VICTORIA CROSS (VC) is the highest and most prestigious award for gallantry in the face of the enemy that can be awarded to British and Commonwealth soldiers. The Border Regiment was awarded five VCs during the course of the First World War.

Abraham Acton (1893-1915) was born in 1893 in 2 Tyson's Court, Roper Street, Whitehaven to Robert and Eleanor Acton of 4 Regent

Acton portrait dated 1916. The artist was John Dalzell Kenworthy (1858-1954).

Award: Abraham Acton's VC. It is displayed at Whitehaven's Beacon Museum. Private Acton's VC was donated to the former Whitehaven Museum (re-housed in the Market Hall in 1974) by his youngest brother, Charles Acton, late father of former Copeland mayor June Pickering.
(Whitehaven News)

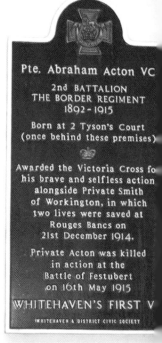

Pte. Abraham Acton VC
2nd BATTALION
THE BORDER REGIMENT
1892 - 1915

Born at 2 Tyson's Court
(once behind these premises)

Awarded the Victoria Cross for
his brave and selfless action
alongside Private Smith
of Workington, in which
two lives were saved at
Rouges Bancs on
21st December 1914.

Private Acton was killed
in action at the
Battle of Festubert
on 16th May 1915

WHITEHAVEN'S FIRST V

WHITEHAVEN & DISTRICT CIVIC SOCIETY

A memorial plaque marks his birthplace in Roper Street.
(Whitehaven News)

Square, Senhouse Street, Whitehaven.

He enlisted at Whitehaven in the 5th Border Regiment (TF) and then transferred to the 2nd Border in January 1914 as a regular soldier. He went to the Western Front with a draft of reinforcements, which included James Alexander Smith (1881-1968), on 25 November 1914. Acton and Smith, born in Workington, were both awarded their VC for their actions on 21 December 1914 at Rouges Bancs, France (about 0.6 miles NNW of Fromelles). They went out from their trench and rescued a wounded man who had been lying exposed to the enemy for 75 hours. On the same day they again left their trench, under heavy fire, to bring in another wounded man. They were under fire for an hour while conveying the wounded to safety.

Of the two men who were rescued in this action, one was from Whitehaven and one from the Carlisle area. The Whitehaven soldier was Private David 'Jimmy' Ross, whose family at one time lived at Rosemary Lane, Whitehaven and who, like Acton, had attended Hogarth Mission (a place of worship that has long since gone). Ross enlisted at the age of 23. He had survived the Wellington Pit explosion in Whitehaven on 11 May 1910 in which 136 men and boys died.

Smith survived the war and lived to the age of 87. Acton was killed in action at the Battle of Festubert, France on 16 May 1915, age 22, and his body was never found. He is named on the Le Touret Memorial to the Missing. He was posthumously honoured with the VC which was presented to his parents by HM King George V at Buckingham Palace on 29 November 1916. Acton was apparently engaged to a local girl when he went to war and she vowed not to marry anyone else until after seven years had passed.

In a letter from his sister Beatrice, written from her home in Peter Street, Whitehaven on 19 May 1915, three days after Acton had been killed in action, she says the family were hoping Abraham would be safely reunited with them soon. She describes their brother Harold, who was only five when his brother was killed, as 'such a little demon, always playing at soldiers, shooting Germans'.

James Smith VC. His birth name was James Alexander Glenn and his VC is displayed at the King's Own Royal Border Regiment and Border Regiment Museum, Carlisle Castle.
(Whitehaven News)

Fighting in the flooded trenches: This 1914 postcard is an artist's impression of trench life on the Western Front in the first winter of the war.

There is also a brass plaque that had been erected at Crosthwaite School in Rosemary Lane where he was educated. The school closed in 1985 and the plaque is now at The Beacon. A memorial plaque also marks his birthplace in Roper Street. He was one of 13 brothers and sisters and worked with his father at Harrington No 10 colliery and also, for a time, at Barrow shipyards.

After the war, Robert and Elizabeth Acton moved to Douglas, Isle of Man where two of their married daughters lived and Abraham Acton is commemorated on St Matthew's Church War Memorial, Douglas. But the memorial has weathered to the point of total illegibility.

Acton, an Orangeman, is also named on the Ulster Tower memorial at Thiepval, France and he is named on a Regimental VC Memorial at Carlisle Cathedral.

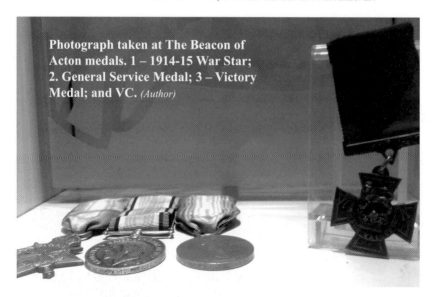

Photograph taken at The Beacon of Acton medals. 1 – 1914-15 War Star; 2. General Service Medal; 3 – Victory Medal; and VC. *(Author)*

What was an English recipient of the VC doing in the Orange Order (a Protestant fraternity based primarily in Northern Ireland)? In Ireland, there were doubts on both sides. Why should the Ulster Volunteers fight against the Kaiser, the strongest defender of Protestantism in Europe? Why should the Irish Volunteers fight for Britain given their efforts to secure Home Rule?

Cumberland was a hot spot for Irish immigration into England in the 1850s. Orange Lodges were organised in Cumberland under the Grand Orange Lodge of England, one such being in Whitehaven, and there were Orange Order marches in Maryport until the 1960s. Both Whitehaven and Cleator Moor, a town based around the iron works industry, had large numbers of both Protestants and Catholics and both towns had deep inter-faith rivalry. Even at weekday masses, St Begh's Catholic Church, Whitehaven routinely had attendances of 1,000 in the 1910s and 1920s (source: The mass books at Whitehaven Record Office).

Chapter Six

The area's gallantry; the VC

PRIVATE JAMES ALEXANDER Smith VC (1881-1968) was born James Alexander Glenn on 5 January 1881 and is thought to have taken his mother's maiden name so he could enlist at the age of 13 into the 3rd Militia Battalion. He served as a regular soldier and was discharged into the Army Reserve but was called up in August 1914 and sent overseas. In March 1915, three months after his courageous acts with Acton, Private Smith was wounded and returned to Workington.

The West Cumberland Times recorded how Smith was given a hero's welcome as he arrived home by the last train from Carlisle:

'That he did not manage entirely to avoid the welcome waiting for him was due to his being "spotted" on the train at Wigton. The news was wired on to Maryport and from Maryport to Workington and when he appeared his modesty was shocked by the reception.'

He was hoisted shoulder high and carried through the streets.

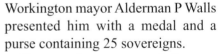

Workington mayor Alderman P Walls presented him with a medal and a purse containing 25 sovereigns.

He served overseas until January 1917, returned to England and was finally discharged on 8 January 1919. After the war, he went to Middlesbrough. He served with the Home Guard during the Second World War and died in May 1968 at his home in Middlesbrough. His medals were bequeathed to the Border Regiment and are on display in the regimental museum at Carlisle Castle. He is named on the Regimental VC Memorial, Carlisle Cathedral.

Tom Fletcher Mayson (1893 – 1958) was born in the village of Silecroft, near Millom.

Border Regiment VC Memorial, Carlisle Cathedral, including Crimean War and Indian Mutiny . *(Cumbria Museum of Military Life)*

He was 23 years old, and a Lance-Sergeant in 1/4th King's Own (KO) Royal Lancasters during the First World War when the following deed took place for which he was awarded the VC. On 31 July 1917 at Wieltje, near Ypres, Belgium, when his platoon was held up by machine-gun fire, Lance-Sergeant Mayson, without waiting for orders, at once made for the gun which he put out of action with bombs, wounding four of the team; the remaining three of the team fled, pursued by Lance-Sergeant Mayson to a dug-out where he killed them. Later, when clearing up a strongpoint, this non-commissioned officer again tackled a machine-gun single-handed, killing six of the team. Finally during an enemy counterattack he took charge of an isolated post and successfully held it until ordered to withdraw and his ammunition was exhausted.

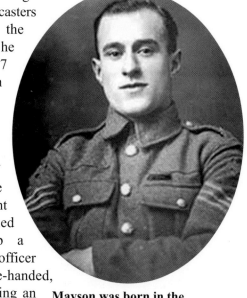

Mayson was born in the John Bull Inn, now a private house.

His VC was left to St Mary's Church Whicham, from where it is on loan to the King's Own Museum, Lancaster. What the citation accompanying the VC doesn't say is that the killing was done by a little man only about 5'5" tall who, apparently, by his own admission, 'was terrified and didn't know what had got into him'. According to those who knew him in later life, he certainly never bragged about his deed, and seemed such a 'quiet little chap'.

In December 1917, he returned to Millom and Silecroft. At a special ceremony in Silecroft, he received a gold watch, chain and medal and an illuminated address. The watch, a handsome demi-hunter, bore a monogram on the outer case, while inside was the inscription, 'Presented to Lance Sergeant Tom F Mayson, KORL Regiment, with hearty congratulations and best wishes from the parishioners of Whicham and Furness on receiving the VC.' The chain, a massive gold cable, carried a choice medallion in gold and enamel of the badge of the King's Own Royal Lancaster Regiment. The 'Silecroft' gold chain and medal were acquired by the King's Own Museum in October 2010 and are on display.

Harry Christian (1892-1974) was for forty years the landlord of the

Chain and medallion presented to Mayson by villagers.

Park Head Inn, Thornhill, Egremont along with his wife Nellie (nee Adams). For many years he kept his VC behind his bar. He was born in 1891 at Wallthwaite, Pennington near Ulverston, where he was brought up and, after several farming jobs, enlisted in the KO Royal Lancasters in 1910 and was posted to India. Having returned to England in December 1914, he was posted to France in February 1915 and won the VC for gallantry at Cuinchy, France on 18 October during the Battle of Loos.

His citation, published in the *London Gazette* on 3 March 1916, read:

'He was holding a crater with five or six men in front of our trenches. The enemy commenced a very heavy bombardment of the position with heavy 'minenwerfer' bombs, forcing a temporary withdrawal. When he found that three men were missing, Private Christian at once returned alone to the crater, and, although bombs were continually bursting actually on the edge of the crater, he found, dug out, and carried one by one into safety all three men, thereby undoubtedly saving their lives. Later he placed himself where he could see the bombs coming, and directed his comrades when and where to seek cover.'

He was subsequently badly wounded and returned home. Still recovering from his wounds, he was presented with his VC in Glasgow in 1917 by King George V. His medal was the first to be awarded to his regiment during the war. On recovery from his wounds, he returned to 2nd KO and served in Salonika, eventually being discharged in 1919. He served his country for nine years.

He died on 2 September 1974 in West Cumberland Hospital, aged 82, and is buried at Egremont Cemetery. His name appears on the War Memorial to those who served but returned from the Great War, which

Harry Christian's gravestone in Egremont Cemetery, North Road, Egremont.

is set into the gable end of Memorial House at Low Mill, Egremont. There are also memorials to him at the Coronation Hall, Ulverston and a bench at Cross-a-Moor crossroads, Pennington. His medals were purchased by the King's Own Museum, where his VC is on display.

At 19, Lieutenant Edward 'Ned' Benn Smith (1898-1940) of Maryport was the youngest soldier of the First World War to be awarded the VC. In 1917, he left his job as a coal miner at the Oughterside Colliery, Aspatria, joining the Lancashire Fusiliers at the age of 18. He is unusual in having gained both the DCM (Distinguished Conduct Medal) and VC, and in quick succession, during the Hundred Days Offensive (8 August to 11 November 1918). He won his VC for action at Serre, France, 21-23 August 1918. The following details were given in the *London Gazette* of 18 October 1918:

> Edward Smith, D.C.M., Lancashire Fusiliers, while in command of a platoon, personally took a machine gun post with rifle and bayonet, killing at least six of the enemy, regardless of the hand grenades they flung at him. Later he led his men to the assistance of another platoon he saw in difficulties, took command, and captured the objective. During the counter attack next day he led forward a section and restored a portion of the line.

When he returned to Maryport in 1919, Smith was greeted by a cheering crowd of 6,000 people.

With the inevitability of war becoming increasingly likely during the summer of 1939, Smith re-enlisted with the Lancashire Fusiliers. He was among the first contingent of the British Expeditionary Force to sail for France.

In the Second World War, he served as quartermaster lieutenant but was killed in action at Bucquoy, France on 12 January 1940, age 41. He had died from injuries caused by a head wound the previous day. It may have been caused by what would in later years become known as 'friendly fire'. He is buried at Beuvry Communal Cemetery Extension, France. His VC is displayed on rotation at The Lord Ashcroft Gallery, Imperial War Museum.

Lance Sergeant George Harry Wyatt VC (1886-1914), the husband of coalminer's daughter Ellen Wyatt (née Graham) of Kells, Whitehaven, was awarded the VC while serving with the 3rd Battalion, the Coldstream Guards at Landrecies, France, in August 1914. On the night of the 25/26 August, he twice dashed out under heavy fire to extinguish burning straw that threatened his battalion's position.

Wyatt was born in Worcester. He had married the Grahams' daughter at Christ Church, Whitehaven in 1912 and the couple had two children. Mrs Wyatt came back to Whitehaven to live with her parents at Kells while her husband was serving abroad. Wyatt was in the Barnsley borough police before the war and Doncaster police after the war, retiring in 1934. He died, aged 77, and is buried at St John's Churchyard, Cadeby, Doncaster. His VC is held by the family.

Ellen Wyatt's brother Private John Graham, 6th Border Regiment, died at Gallipoli on 21 August 1915. He is commemorated on the Helles Memorial, a CWGC war memorial near Sedd el Bahr, Turkey.

Thomas Elliott and James Hartley were nominated for the VC but not awarded the medal. Elliott, who served with the 2nd Battalion Royal Scots Fusiliers, was killed in action on 28 August 1915 at Givenchy, aged 22. He is buried at Cuinchy, France.

He came from Harras Moor, Whitehaven and was mentioned in despatches (MiD). A soldier MiD is one whose name appears in an official report written by a superior officer and sent to the high command, in which is described the soldier's gallant or meritorious action in the face of the enemy. In the British Armed Forces, the despatch is published in the *London Gazette*.

Lieutenant James Hodgson Hartley (1872–1918) was born at Peter Street, Whitehaven and was serving with the Medical Corps attached to the South African Forces when he was nominated for the VC, but he too was 'only' to receive a MiD. The action for which he was nominated for a VC was his involvement in the rescue of six wounded soldiers under heavy enemy fire. Five survived and one man died of his wounds three days later.

Hartley died in South Africa on 27 October 1918, but is not commemorated by the CWGC, nor is he listed on any of the Whitehaven church memorials. He had served an apprenticeship with grocer John Davis at Duke Street and married the eldest daughter of Mr and Mrs J W Williamson of Wellington Row.

Chapter Seven

St Bees School VCs

THERE WERE THREE St Bees School VCs: Captain John Fox-Russell and Richard William Leslie Wain, both from Wales, and William Leefe Robinson. 183 Old Boys and masters of St Bees School were killed

John Fox-Russell (1893-1917), born in Anglesey, was an enthusiastic member of the Officer Training Corps while at St Bees, which he attended between 1908 and 1910. At the age of 16, he began medical training at London University Medical School, his practical training taking place at the Middlesex Hospital, where he joined the University of London Officers Training Corps. By 1913 he had been accepted for a commission with the Royal Welsh Fusiliers (RWF). When war was declared, he was seconded by the army to complete his medical training.

After obtaining his medical degree, he joined the Royal Army Medical Corps in 1916, seconded to the Royal Field Artillery (RFA). He served in France with the RFA, subsequently becoming attached at his own request to his previous regiment and battalion – RWF 1st/6th battalion. He had by then progressed to the rank of Captain and he joined his old regiment in Palestine. During the first Battle of Gaza, which took place on 27 and 28 March 1917, he was awarded the Military Cross for bravery.

A little over six months later, he was awarded the VC (posthumously) for his bravery at Tel el Khuweilfeh, where he lost his life on 6 November 1917 whilst helping his wounded comrades. The *London Gazette* 8 January 1918 reported:

'Captain Russell repeatedly went out to attend the wounded under murderous fire from snipers and machine-guns, and in many cases, when no other means were at hand, carried them in himself, although almost exhausted. He showed the greatest possible degree of valour'.

Fox-Russell is buried at the Beersheba War Cemetery, south west of Jerusalem. A slate plaque now adorns the outside wall of the family home in Holyhead, a memorial to John Fox-Russell and sibling Captain Henry Thornbury Fox-Russell MC (1864-1918). Just days after the Armistice, Henry Thornbury Fox-Russell climbed aboard a Sopwith

Camel aircraft at Hooton Hall Aerodrome, Wirral on Home Service and took off for a solo flight. The aircraft went into a spin and crashed to the ground. He died, age 21.

Richard William Leslie Wain (1896-1917) was born in Penarth, Cardiff. He was educated at St Bees where he was a member of the Officer Training Corps. On the outbreak of the Great War, despite having won a scholarship to attend Oxford University, he joined the TA. He was commissioned into the Manchester Regiment on 16 July 1915 and served in France.

He was 20 and a Section Commander and Acting Captain in A Battalion, Tank Corps when he was posthumously awarded a VC for his actions on 20 November 1917 at Marcoing, near Cambrai, France. His tank took a direct hit killing all but him and one member of his crew. Though severely wounded he rushed an enemy strong point with a Lewis gun capturing it and taking about half the garrison prisoners. His actions allowed the infantry, which had been pinned back by the machine gun post, to advance. He was killed shortly afterwards while continuing to fire on the retiring enemy.

Portrait: Wain fought in the great tank battle in November 1917.

Lieutenant William Leefe Robinson (1895–1918), born in India, was the first person to be awarded the VC for action in the UK and he died of ill-health brought on by his treatment while a PoW in Poland and Germany. He attacked an enemy airship on the night of 2/3 September 1916, and sent it crashing to the ground.

William Robinson was the son of Horace Robinson, who had a coffee estate in Pollibetta, India. He followed his elder brother Harold to St

Tanks were used for the first time on the battlefield of the Somme on 15 September 1916. *(worldwar1postcards.com)*

Bees in September 1909. In a note to his mother, he said: 'I often wonder if I will make a mess of my life—in the way of failing exams I mean—but you mustn't be too hard on me if I do, old mother dear.' No doubt many young men were worrying about their academic performance during 1913. A year later such concerns would be forgotten.

While at St Bees, he became a sergeant in the school Officer Traning Corps. In August 1914, he entered the Royal Military College, Sandhurst and was gazetted into the Worcestershire Regiment in December. In March 1915, he went to France as an observer with the Royal Flying Corps, to which he had transferred. After having been wounded over Lille by a shrapnel bullet in his right arm, he underwent pilot training in Britain before being attached to No 39 (Home Defence) Squadron, a night-flying squadron at Sutton's Farm airfield, Essex.

On 18 July 1915, he survived his first solo flight and on 28 July he qualified for his Royal Aero Club Certificate No 1475 in a Maurice Farman. On 15 September, he gained his 'wings'. On 18

L21 brought down in flames.
(worldwar1postcards.com)

September, he was appointed Flying Officer and seconded to 19 Squadron. He wrote to his mother on 21 October 1915: 'Now I'm going to give you an example of my abominable conceit. The other day it was most awfully windy, and I was the only flying officer allowed to go up—I took a passenger too. What do you think of a pilot who can pilot a machine and passenger through a 45 hour gale!'

On 24 December 1915, he was on loan to No 10 Reserve Squadron, part of the growing network of London defence squadrons for the specific purpose of 'Zepp Straffing'.

On the night of 2/3 September 1916 over Cuffley, Hertfordshire, Robinson,

Robinson survived active service.

Robinson seated in the BE2c 2963: The mechanics hold up the upper wing centre section damaged by his own gun during the attack on SL11. *(From www.worcestershireregiment.com)*

flying BE2c 2963, sighted a German airship – one of 16 which had left bases in Germany for a mass raid over England. The airship was the wooden-framed Schutte-Lanz SL11, although at the time and for many years after, it was misidentified as Zeppelin L21. Robinson made an attack at an altitude of 11,500ft (3,500m) approaching from below and closing to within 500ft (150m), raking the airship with machine-gun fire. As he was preparing for another attack, the airship burst into flames and crashed in a field behind the Plough Inn at Cuffley, killing Commander Wilhelm Schramm and his 15-man crew.

Wreckage of SL11: On 2/3 September, SL11 dropped bombs on London Colney and on flying further south ran into a screen of searchlight beams. Fleeing north, it dropped its remaining bombs in the Enfield area (perhaps as a ballast to enable it to climb higher) but was shot down by Robinson. *(www.worcestershireregiment.com)*

Genuine: A piece of Zeppelin wire, on display at the Imperial War Museum next to Robinson's medals. *(Author)*

This action was witnessed by thousands of Londoners who, as they saw the airship descend in flames, cheered and sang the national anthem. The propaganda value of this success was enormous to the British Government, as it indicated that the German airship threat could be countered.

In April 1917, Robinson was posted to France as a Flight Commander, flying the then new Bristol F2 Fighter. On the first patrol over the lines, his formation of six aircraft encountered the Albatros DIII fighters of Jasta 11. Robinson, flying Bristol F2A A3337, was forced down, and he was wounded and captured, then transferred to the PoW camp in Frelberg, Germany where he attempted to dig an escape tunnel. After the failure of

Robinson leaving Windsor Castle: George V decorated Robinson with the VC at Windsor Castle on 9 September 1916.
(www.worcestershireregiment.com)

the tunnel, he attempted to bribe a guard; the man accepted the offer, but again the attempt failed. He was sent to the underground fortress of Zorndorf, East Prussia, where there was no chance of escape.

On 2 May 1918, Robinson was transferred to a third camp, Clausthal in the Harz Mountains, Germany. Along with two other officers, he was bundled into a train. Immediately an escape was planned. One officer was to distract one of the guards while the other two made a jump for it. The plan was risky, though for one of the prisoners at least it worked but Robinson, furthest from the door, did not make it. Arriving at Clausthal, he met for the first time one of the infamous Niemeyer twins, commandants of Clausthal and Holzminden camps respectively. Heinrich Niemeyer, known to the prisoners as Milwaukee Bill (the brothers had lived in Milwaukee until the US entered the war), took an instant dislike to Robinson, whose reputation had preceded him. Milwaukee Bill seized the first opportunity of getting rid of him. The last camp to hold Robinson was Holzminden in Lower Saxony, Germany. He escaped with another officer but was recaptured and thrown into solitary confinement.

He survived the war but was weakened by lack of food and mistreatment as a PoW and died on 31 December 1918 in Stanmore, Middlesex at the home of his sister, the Baroness Heyking, from the effects of the Spanish flu pandemic. He was buried at All Saints' Churchyard Extension in Harrow Weald, Middlesex. A memorial to him was later erected at Cuffley. There is a memorial to him at Mecara Anglian Church, India.

At the Imperial War Museum: A postcard to Robinson from eight-year-old Florence ('Thank you very much for bringing that horrid Zepp down'). A photo of her is next to the postcard. *(Author, summer 2014)*

Chapter Eight

Bertie Blair

ROBERT 'BERTIE' CURWEN Richmond Blair (1879-1916) DSO, 5th Border Regiment, born in Harrington, is commemorated on Hensingham St John, Hensingham Village and St Nicholas, Whitehaven war memorials, and was buried at Dranoutre military cemetery, Belgium. The Blair family originated in Scotland, had interests in the Harrington iron works and other industries throughout West Cumberland and lived in Richmond Hill, Whitehaven. The Curwen part of his name is because of the close family friendship of the Blairs with the Curwen family, the main land-owning family in the Workington area. (SPL Curwen, Rector of Workington, who returned to Workington on 15 November 1914, had been a PoW in Bavaria since the beginning of the war).

By profession, Robert Blair was a mining engineer and assistant mine manager and was one of the men awarded the Albert Medal – later renamed the Edward Medal (EM) – for the rescue attempt following the Wellington Pit disaster. At the time he went to war in 1914, he was working on the sinking of the new coal mine at Whitehaven, which was to become Haig Pit (closed 1985).

The Blair Sword, awarded to Captain Blair by Whitehaven Borough

Wellington Pit: It was owned by the Whitehaven Colliery Company.
(www.lakestay.co.uk)

Blair sword: Part of the Beacon's collection.
(Whitehaven News).

Council during the First World War, was in recognition of his having being awarded the Distinguished Service Order (DSO) for conspicuous gallantry at Armentieres, France. As the council presented the sword to Blair, they also recognised the parents of Abraham Acton. It was Blair who had recommended Acton to enlist with the Border Regiment as a regular soldier in early 1914.

On one side of the scabbard of the Blair Sword is shown a representation of the DSO medal; the coat of arms of the borough of Whitehaven; the motto: Consilio absit discordia (conciliation without discord); the embossed initials of the recipient; the crest of Clan Blair and its motto Amo probos ('I love the virtuous'); the cap badge of the Border Regiment (Territorial); and a battle scene of an army officer leading his men to victory. On the other side, there's a miniature view of Wellington Pit inscribed and a sailing ship.

On the night of 27 September 1915 at Armentieres, Blair went out with a party of ten to bomb the enemy's trenches. Finding conditions unfavourable, the party lay down and waited about fifty yards from the enemy's wire. Soon afterwards a party of fourteen Germans were seen advancing towards them. Blair held his fire until they were ten yards away when he shot four of them with his revolver. His party accounted for all the remainder except two and returned unscathed. Blair had constantly taken part in arduous and enterprising night work.

There is a report that Blair had been recommended for the VC but there had been insufficient senior eyewitnesses to confirm his deeds (at least one officer of field rank, a major or above, is required as a witness).

On 5 July 1916, the 5th Battalion's war diary goes on to relate how Blair met his end:

'During night of 4th-5th, officers patrol went out … and reported no sign of enemy patrols, but sounds of work indicated great activity in the repair of the enemy trenches. Enemy snipers have shown more activity yesterday and today using dummies and devices for attracting attention, then firing persistently at our periscopes... Transport shelled at Vierstraat at 11.30pm (no casualties.)

'21st July 1916: Machine gun and rifle fire again persistent. A patrol under Captain R.C.R. BLAIR, DSO, went out from (point) D.5. and reach [sic] the German wire, but they could find no Gap.

'They returned about 1.45am owing to bright moonlight fearing that it would expose the patrol. Going out a few minutes later to point out a spot where some small repairs to our own wire could be made in a very little time, CAPT BLAIR was hit by a bullet and died two hours later without regaining consciousness. The loss of such a gallant officer is keenly felt throughout the battalion.'

Brigadier-General Clifford, commanding 140th Infantry Brigade, to which the 5th Battalion was at that time attached, sent messages of condolence: 'I cannot tell you how distressed I am to hear that Captain Blair has been killed. There never was a more gallant officer, and I know what the loss must be to you and your Battalion. Please convey to all ranks my deep sympathy with them in their loss.'

The whereabouts of Captain Blair's DSO, EM and other First World War medals is unknown. He is buried at Drantoure Military Cemetery, Belgium. Next to him in the cemetery lies his cousin, Lieutenant Claude Leslie Blair MC of St Bees. Robert Blair was with Clement Mossop of the Lowther Arms, Sandwith in the exploit that earned Blair his DSO. So was William Ball, a miner's son from Dale Cottage, Sandwith. Robert Blair's full obituary appeared in the *Whitehaven News* on 27 July 1916, and a memorial service was held at St Nicholas Church on 30 July 1916.

Chapter Nine

Whitehaven town war memorials

THERE WAS NEVER a civil parish of Whitehaven – it was always a township; there was no Ecclesiastical Parish of Whitehaven either until the 1970s. The town of Whitehaven nowadays comprises the former township of Whitehaven, the former township of Hensingham and the former township of Preston Quarter. In 1901, the combined population was 21,523. In 2001, the comparable population was 26,070 (the latest year for which figures are available). The substantive part of Preston Quarter had been added to Whitehaven in 1894 and the balance was split between Whitehaven and Rottington in 1934. Hensingham was also abolished in 1934 and split between Weddicar, St Bees and Whitehaven.

The Roll of Honour was an attempt to list all those who had served in the war – not just those who died – giving their addresses, the unit they served with, if they had been awarded gallantry medals, if they had been

Pillar to First World War and Two: With relief carving of a female figure holding a laurel wreath. *(Ian Stuart Nicholson)*

wounded and so on. There are 2,383 names listed on Whitehaven's Roll of Honour, which was published by the Town Council in September 1919. Following three years of research by Ian Stuart Nicholson, who does voluntary work for the Cumbria Archive Service and acts in an official capacity as Archivist for the Anglian parish of Whitehaven, 625 are known to have died (not 314, the figure provided in the Roll of Honour).

When interviewed, he said: 'That figure is still gently rising. Part of the reason for the huge discrepancy is that the names which are on memorials frequently have tenuous links to Whitehaven which means that the net a century later has to be drawn wide. The new list is fully aligned both with local newspapers and with the CWGC lists. The CWGC also has errors as that was compiled in 1922 to 1924. We have a number of instances where a widow is in Whitehaven by that date but the casualty never set foot in the town. He is included on the list as a null entry if he is known to be on another memorial (and that memorial cited) but as a counted entry if he has no other known memorial.'

One of those missed out of the Roll of Honour is Robert Blair. In the Archives, somebody has written his name in pencil on the page where it should have been printed. He may have been omitted because the family lived in Harrington and Hensingham. At that date, Hensingham was not in the Borough of Whitehaven.

There is a lot of duplication on First World War memorials across the town; lots of people are named on more than one memorial. Unlike memorials erected by the CWGC, the majority of memorials in UK towns and villages were erected by local communities, with the funding, construction, design and names collection overseen by a locally appointed committee. Each memorial can remember a victim in a different way; they remember people in all of their variety and, as such, are testaments to the loss felt in many areas of social life.

The tower of St Nicholas' Church stands in the centre of Whitehaven. There has been a church on this site since 1693 (the first church in the town), although the current chapel is the remains of an 1883-built church, most of which was burnt down in August 1971. There are two brass plaques in the church. They were elsewhere in the church until the 1971 fire, from which they were rescued. The names of the victims of the First World War are inscribed on the south side plaque.

There is also a slate plaque in the church grounds (2001), in memory of members of the Royal Antediluvian Order of Buffaloes (RAOB), both past and present, especially those who gave their lives in two world wars

St Begh's Church, 1906: It has served the Catholic community since 1868.

All those named voluntarily joined the Forces. *(Ian Stuart Nicholson)*

(no names listed). The RAOB is a fraternal organisation and there is an RAOB at John Peel Lodge, Whitehaven.

A Whitehaven Catholic Boys' Brigade printed paper form book of remembrance formerly at St Begh's Church, Coach Road, Whitehaven is now at Whitehaven Archive and Local Studies Centre. Some of the casualties on the Cleator Moor Roll of Honour were members of this Boys' Brigade. The memorial scroll, listing forty-four names, has been replaced by a permanent memorial at St Begh's Church, a multi-coloured marble plaque. The inscription reads 'In honoured remembrance of the Catholics of Whitehaven who fell in the European War 1914-1918. May they rest in Peace.'

Thomas Savage is on the St Begh's church memorial and is buried at Whitehaven Cemetery

Marble plaque: This memorial is the replacement for the Catholic Boys' Brigade paper one. *(Ian Stuart Nicholson)*

Private William John Green, 1st Border Regiment, from Whitehaven is on the permanent memorial at St Begh's Church. He was an ostler in the pits and looked after horses in the war. He was killed in action on 11 April 1918 and is also commemorated on the Ploegsteert war memorial in Belgium.

Private Thomas Savage (1896-1918) lived in Bardy Lane, Whitehaven. He signed up to the 2nd Border Regiment when war broke out, following the lead set by his half-brother, Private Michael McCrink and several of his friends from Whitehaven and the surrounding area. Savage was 17 at the time and under the age of enlistment. They then went through to the Regimental Depot at Carlisle with their friends. After some weeks training, Savage and McCrink went to France on 25/26 November 1914 as part of the draft to the 2nd Border Regiment and were in the trenches on Christmas Day 1914 when the famous 'Christmas Truce' with the Germans took place.

The Whitehaven Congregational WWI and WWII memorial. It was moved to the United Reform Church.
(Ian Stuart Nicholson)

Savage served with Private James Briggs, who was one of the soldiers 'shot at dawn' by his own side before the Battle of Neuve Chapelle, France in March 1915. Briggs, 2nd Border Regiment, was executed for desertion on 6 March 1915, and is listed on the Le Touret memorial for the missing, France.

Regimental records show that Savage suffered from frostbite early in 1915 when he was brought back to a hospital in Britain for the first time before being sent back to the Western Front again. He sustained more serious wounds to the leg in 1916 and was brought back to a hospital in Britain again, believed to be in the Gloucestershire area. He died of wounds on 1 December 1918 and is buried in Whitehaven Cemetery. His medals, several photographs and further information about him were donated to the Border Regiment and KORBR Museum at Carlisle Castle. The last of the 44 names on the Boys' Brigade Memorial is that of Private Thomas Hall, 27th Northumberland Fusiliers. He was born at Cleator Moor and his family later moved to Whitehaven. He was wounded on the Western Front, died in hospital at Aldershot and he was buried in Whitehaven Cemetery in November 1918.

The Congregational Church building in Scotch Street (1874-1980) was sold to Whitehaven Corporation and the proceeds used to build a new Church Hall. The United Reform Church, James Street, Whitehaven remains a part of town life.

Inside the United Reform Church is a stained glass window to Sidney Victor Bentley (1892-1916), 6th KO, who died on 10 July 1916 after serving in Mesopotamia. He was the son of Robert and Rhoberta Bentley of Church Street, Whitehaven. There is a window to Sidney Victor Bentley's brother Clayton Moffat Bentley (1898-1937) erected by his widow. There is also an illuminated parchment Roll of Honour to those who served and returned (moved from the Congregational Church).

There is a brass plaque on a wooden backboard commemorating Frederick William Tallentire (-1918), a member of the Royal Army

Medical Corps, 108th Field Ambulance, who was killed in action at Deerlyck aged 22. He was the son of Mrs Jessie Gradwell of Church Street, Barrow and is buried at Ypres, Belgium. The memorial was erected by his comrades.

Lance-Corporal William Henry Holloway (1894-1916), the son of Martin Holloway of Whitehaven, joined the Seaforth Highlanders in February 1915 and was killed in action in the Persian Gulf. Before the war, he was a joiner and cabinet maker. He is commemorated on the Whitehaven Congregational Memorial and Basra Memorial. The Basra Memorial commemorates more than 40,500 members of the Commonwealth forces who died in the operations in Mesopotamia from autumn 1914 to August 1921.

William Holloway. He belonged to a family which has a long association with the Methodist Church.
(Primitive Methodist Magazine 1916)

Lieutenant John Martindale Hall (1897-1916), 3rd Border Regiment, attached 8th Border (Kendal Pals), was killed in the shelling of trenches held by the battalion in the Quarry Post area in front of Aveluy Woods, south of Arras, France on 28 August 1916, aged 19. He was the son of James and Elizabeth Hall of Inkerman Terrace, Whitehaven and he is buried in Blighty Valley Cemetery, located north-east of the town of Albert, Somme. He is remembered on the Congregational and St Nicholas war memorials. The Blighty Valley Cemetery, Authuille Wood was established in July 1916 and was called after the troops' name for the area. As a 'blighty' was a wound which necessitated a return home for treatment, it is perhaps an indication of the ferocity of the war in the immediate area.

John Hannay Ferguson (1898-1915), aged 17, of College Street, Whitehaven was a boy telegraphist listed as not among the survivors of HMS *Natal*, a warrior-class armoured cruiser built by Vickers, Barrow for the Royal Navy. His name is on panel eight of the Portsmouth Naval Memorial, and on the Whitehaven Presbyterian marble plaque. On 30 December 1915 near Cromarty, Scotland, a series of violent explosions tore through the rear part of the ship. She capsized five minutes later. Some thought she had been torpedoed by a U-boat or detonated a submarine-laid mine, but examination of the wreckage revealed that the explosions were internal.

There is a Cumberland Change Ringers' Association memorial inside St John's Church, Hensingham, a wooden board on its original site, to the memory of the Ringers who fell in the Great War. There are names

Hensingham village roadside cross at the entrance to St John's: This represents people who died in the First and the Second World Wars. There are no names given for the Second World War, just an added bronze plaque

from Cleator Moor, Keswick, Carlisle, Cockermouth and Workington.

The church also has a Leonard William Armstrong (1884-1917) stained glass window. Second Lieutenant Armstrong, 3rd Border Regiment, was killed in action aged 30 and is commemorated on the Arras Memorial, France. The *Whitehaven News* on 14 June 1917 includes letters to his family.

Holy Trinity Memorial. Holy Trinity closed in 1947.
(Ian Stuart Nicholson)

The Primitive Methodist Church on Howgill Street, Whitehaven was built in 1859 but it no longer exists. It had a memorial for the Circuit which is now at Cleator Moor Methodist Church. The United Methodist Free Church, Catherine Street, Whitehaven was built in 1836 but used by the Salvation Army for most of the twentieth century. Hensingham Methodist Chapel does have its own war memorials. The First World War memorial is a marble tablet behind the pulpit. The Reverend EF Martin, a Methodist Minister, enlisted under the Derby Scheme.

The large framed paper set in a four-panelled wooden frame was moved from Holy Trinity Church to Christ Church when Holy Trinity closed in 1947, then moved to St James' when Christ Church closed in 1977. The Christ Church Young Men's Bible Class First World War memorial, a bronze plaque in a wooden frame, also moved to St James' when Christ Church closed.

St James' Choir Vestry floor is tiled in memory of James Wightman and John Wightman. John Wightman, who died on 4 April 1918, was in the Machine Gun Corps and is commemorated on the Pozieres Memorial to the Missing, Somme Battlefields.

There is a brass plaque on a wooden backboard inside the church in memory of Lieutenant Leslie Robert Schrader Gunson (1895-1916), Royal Garrison Artillery, a medical student at Edinburgh University. He was the only son of Clara Jane Gunson of Ghyll Bank, Whitehaven and the late John Robinson Gunson.

St James' has windows, unveiled in 1924, to Private Henry Wallace Mulcaster, who was killed in action on 12 April 1917, and Private Thomas Stanley Metcalf (1890-1916), 1st Battalion, Otago Regiment, New Zealand. His parents were William and Mary Metcalf of Victoria Road, Whitehaven.

The Chapel at St James' Church was enclosed as a Chapel in 1921 as part of the War Memorial Scheme for that church. Nowadays, it is usually called the Lady Chapel and its role as a Memorial Chapel has been expanded over the years to include two memorials to the 1947 William Pit explosion and a glass cross of remembrance/peace for 9/11.

The following are commemorated on St James Memorial:

Lance Sergeant Thomas Henry Anderson (1895-1916), 8th Border Regiment, son of Daniel and Mary Ann Anderson of Bransty Villas, Whitehaven, was killed in a bombing raid on 27 April 1916, in the trenches north of Neuville Vitasse. Before joining the army, he was associated with his father in business as a builder and contractor. He is buried in La Chaudiere Military Cemetery.

Private Leonard Jenkinson (1895-1916) was the youngest son of Mr and Mrs John Jenkinson of Whitehaven. He was attached to the 5th Border Regiment and was killed in action in France on 1 October 1916. He was a devoted worker in the Howgill Street Church.

William James McGuffie (1894-1916) joined the 8th KO. A letter from his lieutenant to his parents dated 7 March 1916 conveyed the sad news that he had been killed in action on the Thursday previous. He says in that letter: 'I knew your son to be a good soldier, liked by his comrades, and a good man for work, and I am sorry to have lost him.'

He is buried at Bedford House Cemetery, a CWGC burial ground near Ypres.

There is a Private Walter Pepper, 5th Border Regiment, on the St James First World War memorial. There may have been a family link to Low Nest Farm, Keswick. Many of the German PoWs at Moota in World War Two were out-posted to farms. One of these was a Carl Pettendrup. He was sent to Low Nest Farm to work with the Pepper family. He fell in love with the farmer's daughter, Elsie, and married her and stayed on for the rest of his life as a Cumbrian farmer. Their daughter Alison True still lives there and runs a B&B business at the farm, as did her parents and her grandparents.

William McGuffie, whose grandfather was a preacher with Whitehaven Methodist Church.
(www.myprimitivemethodists.org.uk)

The following are remembered on the Holy Trinity Memorial:

The first Whitehaven casualty of the First World War was Private James Duckworth, 2nd Battalion Lancashire Fusiliers. He was presumed killed on 26 August 1914, age 28. He is commemorated at La Ferte-Sous-Jouarre Memorial, 41 miles east of Paris where 3,739 men of the British Expeditionary Force who died in August to October 1914 are commemorated. He was the son of Ann Jane and the late Thomas Duckworth, of 23 West Strand, but was born at Wigan and enlisted at Bury around 1904. Before then he had been an errand boy with Edward King, grocer of George Street.

Able Seaman George Todd was one of three town men to die on 1 November 1914. He died along with 900 other men when HMS *Good Hope* was sunk at the Battle of Coronel just before 8pm. HMS *Monmouth* was also sunk in the same engagement with the loss of more than 500 lives. Todd is also remembered on the Chatham Naval Memorial, Kent.

The County Secondary School later became Whitehaven Grammar. In 1968, it relocated from its site in the Catherine Street premises to Hensingham (when secondary education was re-organised on comprehensive lines). The school's two war memorials were re-located to St James' Church.

IN HONOURED MEMORY OF THE
FOLLOWING OLD STUDENTS OF
WHITEHAVEN COUNTY
GRAMMAR SCHOOL
WHO MADE THE SUPREME SACRIFICE
DURING THE WORLD WAR 1939-1945

G. ALLEN	L. HORN
J. A. D. APPLEBY	W. H. JOHNSTONE
H. BAWDEN	G. McCLELLAN
W. H. T. BEATTIE	G. MATTINSON
R. BEWSHER	C. MOORE
W. F. BIRKETT	E. MOORHOUSE
J. BIRNEY	S. T. PARK
J. BIRNIE	H. B. PICKTHALL
J. L. BORROWDALE	T. B. PRATT
R. BRADY	W. A. ROBERTS
L. BROWN	G. SCULLY
G. CLARKE	S. SPEDDING
R. K. CROSSLEY	G. R. STEPP
R. W. DARGAVEL	C. THOMPSON
W. V. EDMONDSON	H. TODHUNTER
J. EVANS	A. TYSON
J. B. GILBERTSON	T. VERNON
V. T. GILL	T. WALKER
J. G. GOLIGHTLY	H. WATSON
T. E. HAILE	C. WILLIAMS
J. C. HIGHAM	T. L. WILLIAMS

ELSIE JOHNSTONE   CATHERINE WILLIAMSON
CHRISTINE M. I. KITCHIN

Whitehaven County Secondary School memorial (six names listed). James Bradley, Joseph Cowen (Whitehaven), Bruce Illingworth (Cleator Moor), Matthew H Mossop (Seascale) B Powell Thornthwaite and James Wightman. Cowen, Seaforth Highlanders, was killed in action, aged 22.

Marble plaque: it is on its original site. There is at least one missing name – Robert Rea Ferguson (1875-1917), who died on 8 April 1917 and is buried at Whitehaven Cemetery.

(Ian Stuart Nicholson)

Private Bruce Illingworth (1897-1916), Royal Fusiliers, the son of William Gibb Illingworth of Embleton, Cockermouth, was killed in action, aged 19. He is listed on the Thiepval Memorial to the Missing of the Somme. It is a major war memorial to 72,195 missing British and South African men who died in the Battles of the Somme with no known grave.

Many small places of worship, chapels and missions in Whitehaven have long since disappeared. The Whitehaven Town Mission on Rosemary Lane, founded in 1856 'to promote the extension of evangelical religion, without reference to the denominational distinctions, among the poor and working population of the town', has managed to keep going. It was rebuilt and enlarged in 1919. The rebuild is not known to have had any war link. It was linked to the success of what was by far their longest serving missioner.

The Oddfellows building on Lowther Street, Whitehaven, was demolished in the 1960s, but the Roll of Honour was saved. It is now in the Whitehaven Archive Centre and is a reminder of the fact that these memorials are moved about when buildings are demolished. Several are coming to light now with the renewed interest in the First World War.

The Whitehaven Colliery Mission's First World War memorial went missing when the Mission moved into a new building in the 1960s. The Hensingham Liberal Club's First World War memorial, a marble plaque, was moved to Hensingham Cemetery when the club closed in the 1960s. There was a paper Roll of Honour, framed and glass covered, at the Hensingham Conservative Club (now closed), which turned up at the Beacon in 2015 when it was preparing for a big First World War exhibition. It is a simple brass plaque which says: Erected by the old boys of Ghyll Bank School In Remembrance of Those who gave their lives In the Great War/1914-1918.

The Secondary School Roll of Honour Book is at Whitehaven Record

Office. The Moresby Voluntary Aid Detachment (VAD) Hospital Commemorative Plaque is at the Beacon but is currently unavailable for viewing.

Corporal Jacob Singleton Ewing, 7th Border Regiment, of Scotch Street, Whitehaven was awarded the DCM. The *Whitehaven News* of 4 August 1916 reports:

'A few weeks ago, Corporal Ewing sent a thrilling account of his squad's experiences in repelling a German attack after a mine had been exploded below them, and it is in connection with this exploit that he has been honoured.'

Ewing was an active member of the Whitehaven Miners' Union and a hard worker for the Labour party in the borough. He is not commemorated anywhere in the Copeland area.

The Lonsdale Roll of Honour exists only on the internet (www.border-regiment-forum.com/onthisday). It was transcribed exactly as it was printed in HMSO's Soldiers Died in the Great War, Volume 39, The Border Regiment. The following Whitehaven men are commemorated on the Roll:

Joseph Henry Casson of Peter Street, Whitehaven died aged 27 and is buried at Waggon Road Cemetery, Beaumont Hamel, France.

Sergeant John Grant, 5th Border Regiment, died at home on 1 October 1918 and is buried at Whitehaven Cemetery.

Private Alfred Dale Jackson, son of Henry and Ann Charlotte Jackson of Church Street, Whitehaven, died on 18 November 1916 and is buried at Serre Road Cemetery.

Private Harold Kitchin, son of Tom and Hannah Kitchin of Peter Street, Whitehaven, was transferred to 5th Border Regiment when the 11th was disbanded. He died on 29 September 1918 and is on the Vis En Artois Memorial.

Private Joseph Leo Marshall, son of John and Mary Marshall of Newhouses, Whitehaven, died on 10 July 1917 and is on Nieuport Memorial.

Private John McCluskey, son of John and Ellen McCluskey of Whitehaven, died of wounds of 1 July 1916, aged 24 and is buried in Blighty Valley Cemetery, Authuille Wood.

Chapter Ten

Baden Powell Thornthwaite and John Burney

BADEN POWELL THORNTHWAITE (1900-1935), who is listed on the First World War Whitehaven Grammar School Memorial, has a fascinating story. He is the soldier who came back from the dead. The man who rejoiced in the name of Baden Powell Thornthwaite, and had tried to get into the army at 15 by lying about his age, had not died in the First World War after all, but most likely had deserted. For he was to turn up again 20 years later, in South Africa.

He was born on 26 February 1900, the sixth child of William and Mary, of 24 South Street, Cockermouth, in Christ Church Parish. His father, a draper/ironmonger from Allonby, died on 20 December 1913 aged 52. His mother Mary lived to 93 and died on 14 February 1961. His schooling was at Cockermouth Fairfield Elementary, then Whitehaven Grammar School – then known as Whitehaven County Secondary School – from 29 April 1914 to 31 March 1915. He enlisted at Carlisle as Private 21848 in the 3rd Battalion Border Regiment on 1 June 1915 (aged just 15) and was discharged in Carlisle on 7 July for lying about his age (stated as 19 years and seven months) to the Recruiting Officer. The 3rd Battalion was basically a recruiting and training battalion.

This lad was not easily put off and he re-enlisted as Private 29156 in the 29th Northumberland Fusiliers (the Tyneside Scottish) at their Grainger Street, Newcastle Office on 30 November 1915. This time it took longer for the Recruiting Officer to realise that he had been lied to, but Baden was discharged again on 17 July 1916 (he had given his age as 16 years, one month). Presumably he was excited by the idea of the war and, with his father dead, felt it necessary to bring in an income.

On 17 April 1917, he enlisted in the Royal Marine Light Infantry at Newcastle (service number PO/20011) and was awarded the British War Medal and the Victory Medal, which he forfeited because he deserted. Until 17 October 1917, he was at the Deal depot, and was then transferred to Portsmouth until 17 December 1918. On 18 December 1918, he became an engine cleaner on the *Princess Royal* being promoted to stoker on 1 January 1919. He served on her until 19 April 1919. During this time the ship was part of the guard fleet to the interned German Navy at Scapa Flow, Orkney. He then became SS 120195 in the Royal Navy and served at Victory II from 16 May 1919 to 21 January 1920 (this was a training depot at Crystal Palace in Sydenham, London), then on the *Dublin* to 25 April 1921 and on the *Birmingham* from 26 April 1921 until 3 May 1921 when he deserted at Simonstown Naval Base, South Africa.

In January 1932, the headmaster of Ennerdale School wrote to the then headmaster of the County Secondary School to tell him that Private Thornthwaite had died in France in June 1917 and his name was therefore inscribed on the School War Memorial. (The preceding information comes from Mr Brian Parnaby's History of the School (2007), page 75 and illustration seven). His death was also added to the Admissions Register. Intriguingly, though, it was not added to the School Roll of Honour Book. Also there was a Harry Messenger Thornthwaite (no apparent relation), born at Great Broughton on 24 April 1899 who died in the sinking of HMS *Torrent* on 23 December 1917, having served in the Navy as J31852 since 29 June 1914. He is not on the Great Broughton memorial, possibly because his mother had by then moved to Liverpool and remarried.

Baden Powell Thornthwaite's name next appears on the passenger manifest for the SS *Windsor Castle* of the Union Castle Line arriving in Southampton from Rhodesia on 6 February 1933. This cites his English address as Dennysmead, Morton, Carlisle – perhaps the address of a member of his family – and his occupation as mine owner. Perhaps that was really true, but is more likely to have been another fiction. He also arrived at Southampton on board the *Caernarvon Castle* on 12 March 1934, this time giving his UK address as c/o Barclays Bank, Carlisle. In 1934, he was living with an Agnes (Grieg) Thornthwaite (nee Murray), aged 30. He then departed Southampton on 5 October 1934 as a family with their one-year-old daughter W Ann Thornthwaite. After his death, Agnes and Ann came back to England on the *Usaramo* arriving on 7 February 1936 to stay at the Leinster House Hotel, Russell Square, London. In 1934, Agnes must have returned to Africa promptly as their child was apparently born in Rhodesia on 12 June 1934. It would appear that the marriage was in Rhodesia although it cannot be traced within Consular records. Agnes was from Perthshire, Scotland and died at Aberdeen on 17 May 1950.

Thornthwaite is known to have sailed from Southampton to Cape Town on 19 May 1933 and 5 October 1934 but is otherwise not heard of until his death from natural causes in South Africa on 19 June 1935.

He left all his money, the princely sum of £167/15/1 (equivalent to

Secondary School, Whitehaven: It was opened in 1908 and fees were £6 per annum. It was decided in 2007 to demolish the whole structure and replace it with a Morrisons supermarket. *(Ralph Lewthwaite,)*

£10,500 today), to a William Erskine Gill, which is interesting as both his mother and at least one brother were still alive. The probate record tells us that he died at the Carn Brae Mine, Mazoe, Southern Rhodesia. This is north east of Harare (formerly Salisbury).

The other interesting fact is that Baden is not on the War Memorial of his home town, Cockermouth.

In the First World War, Sergeant John Burney, from Low Harras Moor, Whitehaven served in the 2nd Border Regiment and, later, in the Machine Gun Corps, and he was awarded the Military Medal for Gallantry (MM).

His joint letter with T Lister and I Knowles from the Front appeared in the *Whitehaven News* on 25 March 1915. They describe their action and 'the Germans and the white flag ruse' and sign as 'lads of the gallant Border Regiment.'

John Burney in his First World War uniform.

Burney received his Military Medal on 22 January 1919 from Major Gillam at Carlisle Castle, on the same day as a fellow NCO in the Machine Gun Corps received the DCM. This was Corporal Corkish who, like Burney, had transferred to the MGC from the 2nd Border. The MGC was a corps of the British Army,

Haig Colliery Mining Museum: On the site of the former Haig Pit, which closed in 1986, the winding engine house and headgear are being restored to their former glory. *(www.visitcumbria.com)*

founded in October 1915 in response to the need for more effective use of machine guns on the Western Front.

Burney was forced to sell his medals, including his MM, during the 1926 General Strike so that he could feed his family. When the Second World War broke out, he was working as a coalminer at Haig Pit. On 11 January 1940, the conveyor belt that transported the coal from the coal face to the pit shaft had broken. Burney was one of a team of five men detailed to repair the broken conveyor belt. It was while this work was being undertaken that he suffered severe injuries from which he died. He is buried at Whitehaven Cemetery.

Chapter 11

Memorials, St Bees

IN 1891, ST BEES had a population of 1,311. For a relatively small village, it is a little unusual in having two 'official' village memorials plus additional memorials for St Bees School and Sandwith School.

The First World War memorial in the Priory graveyard adjacent to the lych gate (the position was decided by a vote of relatives of those who had been killed) is the first you come to. Twenty-six men are listed. One was a naval officer, one a merchant seaman, all the rest were soldiers. Second World War names are on a plaque on the retaining wall below.

The St George and the Dragon memorial stands on a prominent site next to the railway station. This was designed and erected by John Danzell Kenworthy, a local artist who lived at Seacroft House. His son Stanley was killed in 1916. Kenworthy thought the official memorial lacked impact and should have been sited in a more visible place, hence he designed the St George sculpture. In addition to the twenty-six names on Collingwood's Celtic Cross memorial, Kenworthy's memorial lists another villager, Private Arthur Taylor, 5th Border, who died at home in 1917. He is buried in St Bees churchyard.

Lance-Corporal William Ball, 5th Border Regiment, of Sandwith was killed in action at Ypres, 1916, aged 23. He was killed by a shell that burst in the trench where he was working, and his death was instantaneous. His grave is in Belgium.

Fred Bell, Royal Naval Reserve, of St Bees, was lost at sea off Ireland in 1915, aged 26. He had been lost on the *Viknor*, mainly used as a cruising patrol ship during the First World War and equipped with armament. She left the Tyne on 28 December 1914 and went missing. The cause of her loss was uncertain, but as bodies and wreckage were washed ashore on the north coast of Ireland, it was presumed that during the recent bad weather she either foundered or, being carried out of her course, struck a mine in the sea which the Germans were known to have laid. None of the 295 crew was saved.

St Bees Roll of Honour plaque inside St Bees Prio
(Ian Stuart Nicholson)

Sank in 1915: She was known as SS *Atrato* of the Blue Star Line between 1888 and 1912, SS *The Viking* between 1912 and 1914 and HMS *Viknor* from 1914-15.

Claude Leslie Blair (1886-1917), Royal Engineers, of St Bees and a pupil at St Bees, was killed in action in Belgium on 16 June 1917, being caught by a shell while walking along a trench. Only a few days before, he had been awarded the Military Cross. By profession, he was an engineer and had worked for the Whitehaven Haematite Iron and Steel Works at Cleator Moor. He was born at Drigg and his address at NAO is given as 37 Crossfield Road, Cleator Moor. He is buried in Dranoutre Military Cemetery, south east of Ypres.

Oswald Rees Keene, 2nd Duke of Wellington Regiment, died of the effects of gas at Ypres in 1915, aged 24. He was the son of the Rector of Gosforth but had been born in St Bees, his father the Reverend Rees Keene having been lecturer at the St Bees Theological College from 1887 to 1895.

Claude Blair took a leading part in all the school games.

Captain Stanley Kenworthy (1884-1916), 17th Manchester Regiment (2nd Manchester Pals), the eldest son of Mr and Mrs Kenworthy of Seacroft, St Bees, was killed in action on the Somme on 1 July 1916, aged 32. He was head of St Bees School and is buried in Dantzig Alley British Cemetery, Mametz, France.

James McKee, 7th Border Regiment, of Sandwith was killed in action in Arras, France on 19 September 1918, aged 28. His brother, Private Charles McKee, was killed in action in the Dardanelles on 9 August 1915. The *Whitehaven News*, 3 October 1918 reported:

> Mr. and Mrs. McKee, 38 Queen Street, Whitehaven, have given six sons to the war. The other sons are Pte. Frank, now in hospital, shot through both legs; Tom, in France; Robert, now discharged and working on munitions; and George, the youngest, now in training in England.

Prominent place: Stanley Kenworthy was popular in the field of sport and as an officer.

Lance Corporal Clement Mossop was brought up at the Lowther Arms, Sandwith. Perhaps business there was on the quiet side, because his father James described himself as 'Innkeeper and Labourer' in the 1911 census return. James had come to Sandwith from Arlecdon, and he and his wife had five children to support: Clement, two older sisters, and a brother and sister younger. Like a number of his Sandwith comrades, Mossop became a Territorial well before the war. At its outset he was called to the Colours, serving under Lieutenant Colonel Dixon of St Bees, and within months he was in the thick of the fighting in Belgium. Amongst his comrades there were William Ball and one of the Stainton brothers from St Bees.

In his book *The Border Regiment in the Great War (1924)*, Colonel Wylly describes a 1915 incident near Hooge:

> 'The 1st/5th Borders had taken part in a successful attack and were consolidating their position when a fine action was performed by an officer and a private of the Battalion. An officer and a corporal of the Royal Engineers had to go across some open ground in rear of our line when the enemy opened machine gun fire upon them. The officer was almost at once killed and the corporal was

wounded. Upon seeing this, Captain R.R. Blair and 1194 Private Mossop of 'A' Company at once went out and brought them in to the cover of a ditch, being throughout fully exposed to the enemy's fire.'

A few weeks later, Mossop, now promoted to Lance Corporal, was in the line at Armentieres. Mossop was not to survive much longer. He was killed at Armentieres in October, aged 25.

Lance Corporal Henry (Harry) Nankivell (1881-1918), 43rd Australian Infantry, died of wounds received in action in France on 4 September 1918, aged 36. He is not commemorated on St Bees war memorials because he had left the village before the war started, and his enlistment was with the Australian Force. In 1891, at the time of the Census, the family lived next to the Post Office (now 121 Main Street). He worked for 18 months at Fairladies farm before seeking a supervisory post at Whitehaven Workhouse.

Henry (Harry) Nankivell.
(www.stbees.org.uk)

The St Bees School war memorial, erected on 30 June 1921, has dedication plaques fixed to each face. The names are on a separate Roll of Honour in the school chapel and include Assistant Naval Clerk Cecil Martin. He died when armoured cruiser HMS *Monmouth* went down. She was sunk at the Battle of Coronel, which took place off the coast of central Chile, on 1 November 1914: 1,570 men were killed. Twenty-one former masters and pupils received the Military Cross.

The Sandwith Roll features the names of all those who served in the First World War and attended Sandwith school in a parish that had a population of 339 in 1891. It was originally housed in the school building which closed in 1938 and was used as a meeting place until the late 1970s, when it was sold to be turned into a private dwelling. It was about this time that the Roll of Honour and two brass plaques (on the wall of the village school) commemorating those who died in the First and Second World Wars went missing and were believed to have been stolen.

In the 1980s, an anonymous caller to Sandwith Post Office deposited the brass plaque commemorating those who had died in the First World War, but it was not until the summer of 2006 when St Bees Church was

The plaque (pictured) is now in St Bees Priory above the Second World War plaque. *(Ian Stuart Nicholson)*

being re-roofed that the Roll of Honour document turned up.

The unveiling of a brass plaque on the wall of the village school on 19 June 1921 was reported in the *West Cumberland News* on 25 June 1921.

A pre-printed form with names hand-written by calligraphy, all in a glazed wooden frame. *(Ian Stuart Nicholson)*

Chapter Twelve

Memorials, West Cumberland A-Z

Arlecdon and Rowrah

As well as the war memorial, there is also a plaque to Privates John Robert Little and William James Little inside the church. John Robert Little, 7th Royal Sussex Regiment, younger son of David and Hannah Little of Arlecdon parish, was killed in action in France on 28 December 1915, aged 34.

Arlecdon parish is mainly made up of three small villages: Arlecdon, Asby and Rowrah and a few scattered houses. Twenty-three young servicemen of the parish lost their lives in the Great War. Arlecdon parish in 1891 had a population of 5,697.

Beckermet

A granite cross was unveiled in August 1920 at St Bridget's Church, Calderbridge. The original inscription, commemorating twelve men from St Bridget's parish who died in the First World War, is on the front of the war memorial. After the Second World War, the names of those from the parish who lost their lives were inscribed on one side of the memorial. St Bridget's parish, Beckermet had a population of 655 in 1891.

There is also a Roll of Honour on the Rood Screen inside St John's Church, Beckermet. At St Bridget's Church, there is also a Roll of Honour and a plaque to Arthur Joseph Steele (1881-1915), East Yorkshire Regiment inside the church. His parents were Reverend and Mrs Steele of Croft Lodge, Beckermet. At Thornhill Cemetery, there is also a civic cross to the dead of Thornhill &

Arlecdon war memorial, to the dead of the First and Second World Wars, takes the form of a Celtic cross with Celtic designs upon the shaft. It is sited in the churchyard of St Michael's. *(Joseph Ritson)*

Thornhill & Beckermet war memorial. *(Ian Stuart Nicholson)*

Beckermet (15 men listed). There is also a plaque on the side of a house at Low Mill, below Thornhill.

Bigrigg

A memorial tablet (brass on wooden backing) was unveiled inside St John's Church in November 1920 and it is still there. There is also the Moor Row Royal British Legion (RBL) memorial inside the church, moved here when the RBL branch closed.

The church, built in 1874, was founded to provide a more local church for the growing communities of Moor Row, Bigrigg, Woodend and Scalegill. *(www.visitcumbria.com)*

In Bigrigg in September 1916, there was an exceptionally large gathering to give a welcome to the returned soldiers from the Front (*Whitehaven News* 28 September 1916).

Braystones

Braystones Tower is a prominent grade II-listed landmark put up to

Prominent landmark: the tower photographed pre-1920 - which locals called Watson's Folly - is now basically gutted and open to the elements. *(Martin and Jean Norgate, 2014)*

commemorate Queen Victoria's diamond jubilee. The original commemorative tablet records the names of the local worthies who were present at its unveiling in June 1897. In 1920, a war memorial commemorating the ten local men who gave their lives in the First World War was added to the tower. It also honours Harry Christian VC. The memorial is still in situ but no-one is responsible for it. In the early part of the twentieth century, owner William Henry Watson briefly turned Braystones Tower into a miniature museum, filled with Stone Age flints, axes and arrow heads drained from nearby Gibb Tarn (and now in the

British Museum). He also positioned two small cannons from the Woolwich Arsenal in London which were used at Waterloo.

The Harrington brothers are on the memorial. Robert Henry Harrington, 11th Border Regiment, died on 18 November 1916 aged 19. He is also on the Beckermet St Bridget's (Calderbridge) War Memorial, and is commemorated on the two St Bees Memorials and the St Bees Priory Roll of Honour. John Harrington, 5th Border Regiment, was killed by a splinter from a shell on 12 April 1917, aged 22. He is commemorated on the Ronville Military Cemetery Memorial 6 at Beaurains Road Cemetery, France. He had previously been employed at the new sinking pit at the Ullbank iron ore mine, Egremont and had previously been gassed. He is also commemorated on the two St Bees Memorials and the St Bees Priory Roll of Honour. They were the sons of Mr and Mrs Harrington of River View, Braystones. Both brothers are also commemorated on the family gravestone in Thornhill Cemetery, Egremont.

Cleator and Cleator Moor

Cleator parish had a population of 9,464 in 1891. In August 1914, St Mary's Catholic Church, Cleator Moor held nightly services for the end of the war. Every seat was filled. A memorial was erected within St Mary's so that the Catholic dead would be remembered in prayers at every mass.

On Cleator Main Street, the war dead were celebrated with a traditional monolith memorial, along with the names of the dead

Focus for everyone: The plinth in The Square, made of iron ore dust and resin, reads To the Glory of God and to remember the sacrifices given by those to all conflicts. *(Ian Stuart Nicholson).*

inscribed throughout its surface. Cleator Moor Wesleyan Methodist Church has a First World War plaque inside. Most writing is in black, with some initials in blue and the names of the casualties in red.

On 13 November 2005, Cleator Moor obtained the Cleator Moor Civic Memorial. The war memorial sculpted by Colin Telfer of Maryport, who worked in Cumbrian coal pits for more than 20 years, was the first memorial dedicated to all the townsfolk in one place. It depicts a nurse treating a seated wounded soldier in First World War uniform. It was decided not to put any specific names on the memorial, for various reasons. For example, sometimes a person is accidentally missed off any such list. Also, it was decided that although most people still focus on the world wars, particularly at Remembrance time, the memorial should be dedicated in such a way that it commemorated the sacrifices made in all conflicts. But a Roll of Honour to accompany this memorial was published in summer 2012. It adds new names previously omitted from the existing memorials as well as correcting various historical errors. New names are still being found.

The Cleator Moor Co-operative Society also remembered those who volunteered to serve their country during the Great War. Its employees were remembered in a Roll of Honour.

Lance Corporal H Pearson of Cleator Moor had filled the office of President of the Cleator Moor Co-operative Society. Prior to enlistment, he was 27 and was employed by Moresby Colliery Company. The Co-op Roll of Honour is known to have been produced mid-war and not later updated – the inscription does not even give the end date of the war. No-one seems to

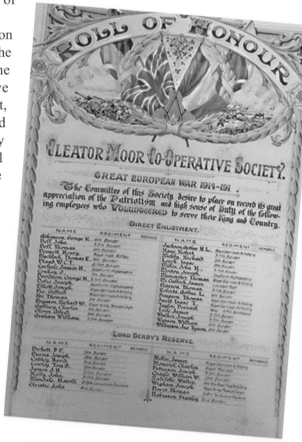

Beautifully designed: The Roll of Honour is now in Cleator Moor Library.

(Jospeh Ritson)

Peter Kennedy is buried in the Hargicourt Communal Cemetery Extension. *(Joseph Ritson)*

know at what stage in the war, and nor does it state who were the casualties. So Pearson likely joined up after the Roll of Honour was produced. He is on the St John's Church Memorial.

Other memorials at Cleator Moor include one outside at St John's Church, Free Churches (Methodist Church), Peter Joseph Kennedy and Peter Joseph McNamee. There are also the altar rails at St Mary's RC Church, Cleator Trumpet Terrace Memorial, stained glass windows and a brass in St Leonard's (and also a missing Roll of Honour).

Private Peter Kennedy (1893-1917), Tyneside Irish, enlisted in Cleator Moor. He died on 29 August 1917, aged 24, in the Hargicourt area. His Medals Rolls index card simply states killed in action (the Medal Rolls Index is the listing of 4.8 million individuals who fought in the First World War). Lance Corporal Peter McNamee, Tyneside Irish, was killed in action on 13 August 1916, aged 19.

Private John Jackson of Cleator Moor drowned on passenger ship RMS (later HMT) *Royal Edward*, aged 24. She belonged to the Canadian Northern Steamship Company and was sunk by U-14 on 13 August 1915 with a large loss of life while transporting Commonwealth troops. JB Jackson is listed on the St John's Church memorial.

The *Whitehaven News* of 24 January 1924 reports on the military wedding at Cleator of Lieutenant CH Walker MC, 2nd Border Regiment and Miss Queenie Walker of Bigrigg. The best man was Lieutenant Colonel Forbes Robinson VC. During the war, Walker – the son of Canon Walker, Rector of St Paul's Church (1898-1936), Causewayhead, Silloth – served with the Lonsdales.

Distington

There are three First World War memorials in Distington, in a parish that had a population of 1,819 in 1891: Distington Brass; Distington Village;

Distington stained glass; and Arthur Murdo Maxwell Robertson-Walker.

The Church of the Holy Spirit has two brass plaques inside, one for each war, on a combined piece of wood. There is a stained glass inside remembering Captain Percy Dickson Robinson, Royal Flying Corps, and Second Lieutenant Thomas Vivian Robinson, Royal Flying Corps. There is also a brass plaque remembering Captain Arthur Murdo Maxwell Robertson-Walker (1880-1916), 8th Battalion Royal Fusiliers, who was killed in action at Ovillers, France on 7 July 1916, aged 36. The tablet was erected by his family.

There is a granite pillar in Distington Village, south end of Main Street. It commemorates fifty-three people who died in the First World War and twenty-one from the Second. It was dedicated on 16 April 1921 by Major CA Vallentine TD of Ellerkeld, Workington and moved very slightly to the current location in 2001 due to road improvements.

Egremont

Egremont parish had a population of 6,258 in 1891. The memorial in Market Street (above) was unveiled in June 1922 by Harry Christian VC. A service of dedication then took place, followed by a parade of serving soldiers and a large contingent of demobbed soldiers led by the town band.

The Great War names are set around the upper portion of this roadside memorial in Market Street. The top is surmounted by a life-size bronze of a First World War infantryman leaning on a rifle.
(Ian Stuart Nicholson)

Cumberland industries: Clintz Quarry is now a nature reserve.
(Andrew Smith)

The name of Private Joseph Varah, Border Regiment, is included on the memorial. He was killed in action on the Somme in 1916, aged 27. Prior to enlisting (26 September 1915), he was employed by the Moss Bay Company at Clintz Quarry (limestone; it closed in 1939), Egremont. He was from St Bees but a resident of Egremont at the time of his enlistment.

Egremont Wesleyan Methodist Church has a First World War memorial, an oak board. It is in the upper room of the Methodist Church, Main Street and mentions the fallen and those who served. There is a wooden First and Second World War memorial board also in the upper room of the Methodist Church – it was in the old Castle Methodist Chapel until closure in 1962. There is also a brass memorial in Egremont Parish Church.

High Mill, Egremont – originally a paper mill – was bought by the Wyndham Mining Company and used as a store and offices. They leased part of the mill to the Territorial Forces during the Great War. And the 'Filling Station' of Henry Graham was built in 1962 on land that had been used during the Great War as an encampment for American soldiers billeted in large wooden huts.

Corporal Robert Walker Clements, 5th Border Regiment, of Brisco Mount, Egremont was awarded the Military Medal in 1917. The *Whitehaven News* of 18 January 1917 reported:

Personal risk: Clements rescued a friend. *(Cumberland News)*

'Corpl Clements was instrumental in rescuing a chum who had been partly buried by a shell. To do this they had to go into the open and at great personal risk brought their chum back.'

Bob Clements and his wife had one child and she died in 1919, aged 14, while they were living at Bigrigg. He survived the war and died in Egremont in 1979.

Ennerdale

The Ennerdale Parish War Memorial near Cleator lists the names of fallen parishioners of the world wars. It is found in the churchyard of St Mary's, Ennerdale, in a parish (Ennerdale and Kinniside) that had a population of 519 in 1891. There were two sets of brothers killed out of a casualty list of seven, Private Henry Brown (1898-1916), 1st Border Regiment, and Private William Brown (1895-1915), 7th Border, and Lance Corporal Thomas Mackin, 1st/5th Border, and Lance Corporal John Mackin, 2nd Border. Henry Brown died of wounds at home. William Brown, who lived in Frizington, was killed in action.

After the First World War, Britain experienced a severe shortage of timber. Thousands of trees, mainly Sitka spruce, were planted on the slopes of Ennerdale changing the ancient medieval landscape forever and creating, as writer Alfred Wainwright (1907-1991) described, a 'dark and funereal shroud of foreign trees'.

World War Two names were added and the memorial rededicated on 10th April 1949.

(Ian Stuart Nicholson)

Eskdale Valley Memorial

This memorial is at the junction of Beckfoot to Boot Road and Stanley Ghyll Force road, opposite the former Low School, Boot, Eskdale. It includes Tom Fossey who was presented with a £10 cheque as the first Eskdale man to enlist for foreign service as reported by the *Whitehaven News* of 5 November 1914.

There is also a stained glass window to Siegfried Herford (1891-1916) at the Outward Bound. Private Herford of 24th Battalion Royal Fusiliers died from a grenade blast in the trenches of Flanders on 28 Februrary 1916, aged 25. He is buried in Brown's Road Military Cemetery, Festubert, France. He is also commemorated on the Great Gable War Memorial.

He was the son of Charles H and Marie Catherine Herford (nee Betge) of Parkfield Road, Didsbury, Manchester. His mother came from Bremen, Germany and it is believed that the marriage took place there as it cannot be traced in British records. His father Charles (1853-1931) was Professor of English Literature at Manchester University and was at least second generation British. He belonged to the large Teutonic population of Manchester, many of whom were Unitarian, as were the Herford family.

So how is there a window to him in Eskdale? Originally it was in 'a Chapel' in Manchester. Almost certainly this was Cross Street Chapel, Manchester. This was, and is, the main Unitarian Church in central Manchester. The chapel was destroyed in the Second World War Blitz and subsequently rebuilt.

Second Lieutenant Strathern of 3rd Yorkshire Regiment (attached to 2nd Border), the son and only child of William and Margaret Strathern of Eskdale, is remembered on a choir stall at St Catherine's Church, Boot. He died on 8 July 1916 on the Somme, aged 28. He is also commemorated on the Thiepval Memorial.

We think of the years of the Great War as being years of misery and austerity, yet rich eccentrics could still afford to play. One such, the model maker Wenman Joseph Bassett-Lowke (1877-1953), had been running a miniature railway line in his garden at Irton Hall, Holmrook. He decided that the Eskdale railway line would provide him and his friends with even more fun. By 1916, the re-gauged track (15in/381mm) ran as far as Irton Road, and the following year these miniature trains were running the full length of the line. His close contacts with German toy manufacturers, particularly Gebruder Bing, introduced him to the very advanced state of design in Germany and organisations such as the Deutscher Werkbund. He was quick to join its British equivalent, The Design and Industries Association, founded at the opening of the Great War.

Frizington

Frizington Village memorial is a granite pillar within a gated enclosure and remembers those who died in the First World War, the Second World War and the Korean War (1950-1953). It was initially dedicated to commemorate the fifty five casualties of the First World War

St Paul's Church, Frizingon has a brass plaque with names in three columns all set in a wooden frame. At the top are two angels holding a scroll in which is inscribed the dedication to the men in the parish who fell in the Great War.

St Joseph's Roman Catholic Church, Frizington has a freestanding memorial outside. It commemorates the members of the parish who gave their lives in the First and Second World Wars.

Private Peter Kervin, 5th Border Regiment is buried in St Joseph's cemetery and named on the Frizington Village memorial. He died aged 43 at home on 31 January 1917 after sustaining wounds at Loos in September 1915. He was given a full military funeral. A military funeral may feature guards of honour, the firing of volley shots as a salute, drumming and other military elements, with a flag draping over the coffin.

Private Jacob Lavery, 2nd/5th Border Regiment, of Frizington was one of seven brothers all in the Border Regiment: Corporal Alex Lavery, 10th Border, Private David Lavery, 9th Border; Private Issac Lavery, 3rd Border, Sergeant Joseph Lavery, 9th Border; Private William James Lavery; 3rd Border, and Private John Lavery, 9th Border. Only Alex Lavery died; the other six survived. He must have moved to Hensingham as he is on both the Frizington and Hensingham Memorials.

Gosforth Village memorial to the First World War is in Main Street. There are no names on it. *(Ian Stuart Nicholson)*

Gosforth

The parish of Gosforth had a population of 1,021 in 1891. There is also a memorial, a white marble plaque on a grey marble backboard, inside St Mary's Church, Gosforth.

Gosforth still holds an agricultural show in August. It ceased for the duration of the First World War. The two fields adjacent to Gosforth Hall was the site of the show from 1876 until 1913. On the revival of the show in 1919, a new showground was found at Harecroft Park on the opposite side of the road to Harecroft Hall. In September 1917, the Eskdale Show was cancelled due to war.

Great Gable

The Great Gable (a mountain in the Western Fells) memorial was officially unveiled before 500 people who assembled on the summit on Whit Sunday, 8 June 1924.

It was unveiled by Dr Wakefield, President of The Fell & Rock Climbing Club (FRCC) of Great Britain to the memory of twenty of its members who were killed in the Great War. The dedication was read by the Quaker Geoffrey Winthrop Young (1876-1958). During the war, as a CO, he was active in the Friends Ambulance Unit (FAU). He received several decorations, but on 31 August 1917 an explosion caused injuries

The commemoration of the dead on Great Gable. *(FRCC archives)*

requiring the amputation of one of his legs. He continued climbing for a number of years, using a specially designed artificial leg. At the outset of the ceremony, the Union Jack that flew from HMS *Barham* at the Battle of Jutland enshrouded the bronze tablet. At the conclusion, the Last Post was sounded by two buglers of the St Bees School Cadets.

In 2014, the original plaque was replaced and the Royal Engineers helped the FRCC with the tricky task of installing the new one.

Haile

There is a report in the *West Cumberland Times* on 25 September 1920 about the unveiling of the tablet, a marble plaque, in Haile Church near Egremont. Haile parish had a population of 248 in 1891.

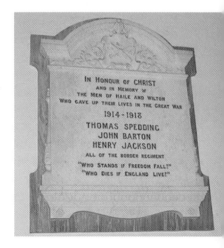

Haile Church war memorial: In memory of Thomas Spedding, John Barton, Henry Jackson (all of the Border Regiment). *(Ian Stuart Nicholson)*

Lamplugh

Lamplugh's memorial to the dead of both world wars stands outside St Michael's Church. It was first dedicated in 1921, listing the names of thirty casualties of the First World War. This was reported in the *Cumberland News* on 22 June 1921. Lamplugh parish had a population of 1,189 in 1891.

Lowca

The Lowca village war memorial is situated close to the main road passing through the centre of the village. There are fifteen names listed: ten from the First World War and five from the Second World War.

Private George Edward Whitehead, who had a Lowca address, does not appear on the war memorial. However, his funeral was reported in the *Whitehaven News* on 5 December 1918:

> 'Private George E Whitehead late of Green House Lowca was badly "gassed" in France and brought home to hospital. On his convalescence he was sent to work at Winngates Farm, Hutton Roof. There he fell victim to influenza and died on Saturday 16 November. His body was brought home to Lowca on Monday 9 November by motor car and interred on Thursday last in Moresby churchyard. A sergeant and six men of the Agricultural Company at Carlisle bore their comrade's body to its last resting place. A hymn was sung at the house before the cortege started, and also at the service in Moresby Church, during which a brief consolatory address was given on the Christ-like self sacrifice of those who have laid down their lives for us.'

The newspaper reported on the same page:

> 'More deaths from the epidemic at Egremont. The grim hand of the Reaper continues to claim toll, young, old and middle aged alike being called.'

This may be the reason why Whitehead's name does not appear on the war memorial as he did not die in battle or from obvious wounds. The fact that he had been badly gassed, however, is likely to have contributed to his death and the funeral address suggests others shared this view. The farm where he died is likely to be Whin Yeats, Newbiggin, Carnforth.

Millom

The Millom War Memorial, built opposite the railway station, was unveiled on 23 May 1925 and the official present at the unveiling was

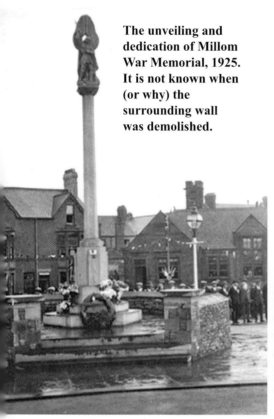

The unveiling and dedication of Millom War Memorial, 1925. It is not known when (or why) the surrounding wall was demolished.

The unveiling and dedication of Millom War Memorial, 1925. General Sir Louis Vaughan can be seen, as can the memorial's sculptor, Alec Miller (second from right).

Major General Sir Louis Vaughan (1875-1942). He was born in Millom. One man listed is Millom vicar's son Second Lieutenant Frank Guy Buckingham Pascoe, the rear seat observer in a wood-and-canvas aircraft called an RE8. Lieutenant Pascoe and his pilot Sergeant Hubert Whatley were killed on 2 July 1917 when the plane came down in a ball of flames at Deulemont, France.

The *Millom Gazette* of 29 May 1925 reported:

'Major-General Sir Louis Vaughan saluted the Memorial, then turning to his hearers immediately facing the front view of the structure, he said: "We have assembled here today on this solemn occasion to unveil and dedicate this beautiful memorial to those gallant sons of Millom who gave their lives to their country during the Great War. In 1914, when hostilities broke out, the men of Millom were amongst the first to come forward and offer their services to their country, and during the succeeding four-and-a-half years every man in the nation was called upon to do some task for the great Empire to which we have the honour to belong."

'Councillor Youren, Chairman of the Council, said it was with mingled feelings that he accepted the Memorial on behalf of the inhabitants of the town. He regretted that civilisation had not so far advanced as to make war an impossibility, and that more peaceable and more conciliatory methods had not been adopted to settle the grievances and disputes of nations without resorting to the follies and arbitrament of war. At the same time he rejoiced to know that, when the call came to the manhood and the womanhood of the country and liberty, so many of our own townspeople answered the call of duty.'

By the late 1980s, the original sandstone panels had become weathered and were difficult to read. Replacement panels were commissioned by the town council, but some spelling mistakes were introduced on to them by the contracting monumental masons.

Lance Corporal Jonathan Whitehead Mason, of the 21st Division Cyclist Company, Army Cyclist Corps, had been discharged from the Army (19 June 1916) as no longer physically fit for war service. He committed suicide at home in Lonsdale Road, Millom on 13 July 1917, aged 22; he was found hanging in a stable adjoining the house. He was eligible for award of the 1914-15 Star, the British War Medal and the Victory Medal. Additionally, he had been awarded the Silver War Badge in recognition of an honourable discharge as a consequence of his wounds. He is listed on the Millom War Memorial, but was not entitled to be commemorated by the Commonweath War Graves Commission (CWGC).

The *Millom Gazette* of 12 July 1918 reported that the Coroner said

SS *Cambria*: the ship that brought Jonathan Mason home from France.

this was an especially sad case because the deceased was a fine young man who had done his best to assist his country in its time of need. In August 1914, he was wounded in action by shrapnel and also had a gunshot wound in the head. He was seriously wounded in the head twice and had many other wounds. In reply to the Coroner, his father, an ironworker of Lonsdale Road, said his son did not show any horror of the war, but it had a

The Masons: Jonathan's sister Katherine.

terrible shock upon him. Jonathan's sister Josephine said he spoke of his experiences of the war and the wounds he had received, and seemed alarmed about having to join up again. He had been called up for medical examination at Lancaster by the government. He told his father he was 'going to work on a bit'.

The Coroner said the jury had very plain evidence before them. This young man never exhibited any strangeness of demeanour, but it was evident his mind had been very much distracted by the wounds he had received, and being called up to go through a similar experience again had broken down his mind, and caused him to commit this rash act, not with any wilful intention of wickedness to himself, but he was in such a state of mind at the time that he did not know what he was doing. The Coroner suggested that deceased committed the act whilst in a state of temporary insanity.

At the appointed time of the inquest, two of the jurors were absent and the coroner said he would have to resort to the practice of fining them. A juryman said that 9.30am was a somewhat unusual time. The coroner said he did not think the people of Millom were such sleepy folk that they could not get up by 9.30am.

Mr and Mrs Mason lost three sons within 18 months. George Mason, aged 19, employed at Vickers, suffered an instantaneous death in an accident in the new shell shop. He was a machine man and his head was nearly severed in the accident. Corporal Thomas Mason, aged 27, KO, died in hospital as the result of injuries received upon the railway line at Plymouth. He seemed to have attempted to take a short cut across the line. He was in the Millom Territorials when war broke out and was later discharged as medically unfit. He re-joined, only to meet the sad fate.

Rifleman Bernard James Tyson, 1st/6th (Rifle) The King's (Liverpool Regiment) was killed in action on 8 August 1916, aged 23, near Waterlot Farm during the Battle of the Somme and is commemorated on the Millom War Memorial . He was the elder son of Mrs Tyson and the late Mr Daniel Tyson, for many years proprietors of the Wastwater Hotel, Wasdale Head.

Also in Millom, there is a memorial to both world wars at Holy Trinity Church. Millom Wesleyan Methodist Church has a brass plaque on a wooden backboard, there is a First World War pillar and sculpture at the junction of Cambridge Street and Duke Street, a plaque in St George's Church, a marble plaque in Our Lady and St James' Church, and a plaque to George Mason Park in Holy Trinity Church (which was in Kirksanton Chapel until it closed in 1951).

Moor Row and Scalegill
The Moor Row and Scalegill War Memorial is located in the centre of the village and commemorates the villagers who died in the two world wars. There are forty-two names listed on the memorial from the Great War. These are engraved on the other three faces of the plinth. Three have the surname Irving and there is a Dr J James.

A First World War plaque and Roll of Honour were lost when Moor Row Wesleyan Methodist chapel closed in 1969.

There is a London and North Western Railway (LNWR) memorial at Moor Row Working Men's Club. Formerly, Moor Row was at a railway junction which was used for passenger and goods traffic. In the latter half of the nineteenth and the early part of the twentieth century, Moor Row became the new home for many former Cornish mining families.

Muncaster War Memorial, Ravenglass
There are thirteen names on the memorial for those lost in the Great War. After the Second World War, an additional seven names were added of those who had lost their lives in that conflict.

Private William Cowan (1894-1916), 1st Border Regiment, son of RH and Elizabeth Cowan of Ravenglass, is listed. He was the eldest of twelve children, and joined up with his brothers. He was first wounded in 1916 and on his recovery he returned to his battalion. He was wounded again during April1917, suffering from shrapnel injuries whilst sleeping in his dug out. He succumbed to these wounds on 5 May 1917,

Architect Edwin Lutyens was appointed by the Duff-Pennington family of Muncaster Castle to design Muncaster War Memorial, Ravenglass. *(Ian Stuart Nicholson).*

ten months after his younger brother Bob was killed. He is buried at Faubourg d'Amiens cemetery, Arras. Bob Cowan, who enlisted as a Kitchener volunteer in the newly-formed 8th Battalion in 1914, was remembered by his surviving brother Ben as a daredevil who looked for challenge and adventure. He was a sniper in the Border Regiment and went missing, presumed killed, on 5 July 1916. His body was never recovered and he is remembered at Thiepval in France and at Muncaster war memorial.

In August 1914, the Holmrook and Ravenglass rifle club offered free instruction at Holmrook (see WN of 27 August 1914, if you can enlist, you can learn to shoot).

Muncaster Castle's war memorial

The war memorial is to be found within St Michael's Church in the grounds of Muncaster Castle in the form of a plaque within the church. It reads 'Sacred to the memory of Henry Birkett, 2nd Lieutenant, Royal

Private William Cowan.
(BBC)

Air Force of the Schoolhouse, Muncaster … Also his comrades from this parish'.

Birkett, born at The Schoolhouse, Muncaster where he lived with his parents, enlisted with the East Yorkshire Regiment, but was with No 3 Flying School of the newly-formed Royal Air Force (no longer the Royal Flying Corps) when killed in a flying accident at Sedgeford, Norfolk on 24 October 1918, aged 19. His airplane was an Avro 504K (E3445), one of the most prolific and versatile aircraft of the time, used throughout the Great War – and which was still being built until 1932.

Buried in St Michael's Churchyard but not on the adjacent memorial in the church is Corporal Alfred Jerome Vassalli (1881-1914). He had

The headstone of Henry Birkett. His funeral service and burial took place in St Michael's Church and churchyard on 29 October 1918.

been an officer in the Merchant Service, and was training with the Naval Reserve when the Boer War broke out. He joined up and was in the Navy at the Relief of Ladysmith and took part in operations in the Transvaal, Orange Free State and Natal (and was awarded the Queen's Medal with five bars). He was also a despatch rider for General Bethune, in whose cavalry regiment he later served.

Airplane. Avro 504k (E3445).

He was then a Naval Reservist. He was called up at the outbreak of war, but failed his medical. Keen to serve his country, he then joined the King Edward Horse and was promoted to Corporal but his health broke down. He died in King Edward VII Hospital, London on 1 October 1914 from pneumonia contracted while in camp at Slough. He was a Rural District Councillor at Drigg. He is named on the First World War brass memorial inside Drigg Church, Drigg. He married Anne Pembroke (1879-1956) of Derwent House, Drigg, and had three children.

Vassali was buried in St Michael's churchyard in a funeral service on 5 October 1914 conducted by the Rev George Southey Pardoe, then vicar of St Michael's, assisted by Canon Pughe, vicar of Drigg.

Vassalli's gravestone at Muncaster. *(Muncaster Castle).*

Alfred Jerome Vassalli was born in Whitby and educated in Scarborough.

Parton

There is a war memorial at Parton Parish Church, on the main road by the church but well away from any village. Parton (and Moresby) Village Memorial outside Parton railway station is a granite six-sided cross remembering both wars: forty-five residents were killed or missing in the First World War. The *West Cumberland Times* on 8 November 1921 reports on its unveiling. The parish of Parton had a population of 1,452 in 1891.

Victory is in the kitchen mug: Parton victory mug.

(Photo taken at Beacon museum by author, summer 2014).

Private Robert Richard Nicholson from Low Moresby was killed while dressing the wounds of a comrade, and is named on the Parton and Moresby Village Memorial.

There was a First World War memorial at Parton Methodist Church, a small chapel which was closed and sold in 2004. The memorial fell to pieces when it was removed from the chapel wall. It listed Private Thomas Bewsher; Thomas Campbell; Alexander Munro; James Nelson; Anthony

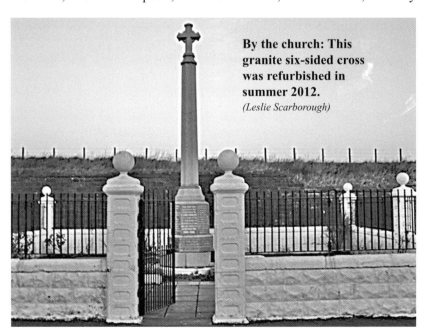

By the church: This granite six-sided cross was refurbished in summer 2012.

(Leslie Scarborough)

Graham; James Mitchell; John T Nelson; and Charles W Sanderson.

Ponsonby
A First World War marble tablet was unveiled on 7 November 1920 inside Ponsonby Church, in a parish that had a population of 169 in 1891. There is a Roll of Honour covering both world wars inside the church. Five men appear on this Roll of Honour.

Scafell Pike
On 10 September 1921, four men carried a war memorial to the top of Scafell Pike. Its inscription reads:

> IN PERPETUAL MEMORY OF THE MEN
> OF THE LAKE DISTRICT WHO FELL
> FOR GOD AND KING, FOR FREEDOM
> PEACE AND RIGHT IN THE GREAT WAR
> 1914 - 1918.
> THIS SUMMIT OF SCAFELL
> WAS GIVEN TO THE NATION SUBJECT
> TO ANY COMMONERS RIGHTS & PLACED
> IN THE CUSTODY OF THE NATIONAL TRUST
> BY CHARLES HENRY, BARON LECONFIELD, 1919

Seascale
There is a bronze plaque inside St Cuthbert's Church in memory of Sergeant Matthew Hudson Mossop of the 15th West Yorkshire Regiment (Leeds Pals) who lived at Laurel Bank, Seascale. He was killed on 1 July 1916 at the Battle of the Somme, aged 26, and is buried at Serre

Seascale Village Cross, outside Seascale Church, lists 11 men. It was executed by Mr Preston, sculptor of Whitehaven and unveiled on 22 May 1921. *(Ian Stuart Nicholson)*

Road Cemetery No 1, France. Also in St Cuthbert's is a copper plaque on wooden backboard in memory of the twenty-one old boys of Seascale Prepatatory School (now closed) who fell in the Great War.

There is a bronze plaque that today is found in the entrance hall of the Gosforth Road School but originally came from the old school on Hallsenna Road and referred to its former pupils. This shows that eighty-six men from the village went to the war, of whom fifteen gave their lives. The village contained only 128 families in 1911.

Never to forget: This model of Seascale Village, c 1914, was made in 2014 to remember the war and was moved to Seascale library. Seascale's Cubs and Beavers produced a poster with the village's war heroes' names on it. *(Seascale Magazine)*

There are a number of other First World War casualties with connections to Seascale who are not listed on one of the aforementioned memorials. These include Gunner Herbert William Bewley (died 1918), son of Thomas and JA Bewley of Seascale; Lance Corporal Postlethwaite Bibby (died 1916), son of William Bibby of Seascale and husband of Annie Bibby of Whitehaven; and Private Arthur Gibson (died 1916), son of Frances Mary Gibson of Seascale.

Wasdale

The East Window behind the altar at St Michael and All Angels Church, Nether Wasdale is dedicated to four local men who fell during the Great War: Joseph Cowperthwaite, 5th Border Regiment who was killed in France in 1917, George Cowperthwaite; Private Hugh Roes Park (died 1916), Westmoreland and Cumberland Yeomanry; and Walker Knight Roper, Westmoreland and Cumberland Yeomanry. Park died at home of tuberculosis contracted in the trenches. He had a brother John in the same regiment. Roper died of diphtheria on 13 April 1916.

A shelter in Nether Wasdale is a war memorial that features no names. *(Ian Stuart Nicholson).*

Inside St Olaf's, a 16th century church at Wasdale, is the Napes Needle window that carries the inscription 'I will lift up mine eyes unto the hills from whence cometh my strength' as a memorial to members of the Fell & Rock Climbing Club who died during First World War.

I WILL LIFT UP MINE EYES UNTO THE HILLS FROM WHENCE COMETH MY STRENGTH.

Chapter Thirteen

Railwaymen Remembered

An instruction was issued in February 1915 that railwaymen were not to be accepted into the armed forces without a signed certificate from their local management effectively agreeing to their volunteering for service. Nevertheless, by the first anniversary of the start of the war, well over ten per cent of those who were railwaymen in August 1914 were now to be found in the army or the navy.

By October 1916, the railways nationally had released 119,600 men for military service, but about as many men had also left for other essential work, including the manufacturing of munitions. By Armistice Day, 184,475 men from the railway companies had entered the armed forces, equal to forty-nine per cent of the number of railwaymen of military age (18-45) on 4 August 1918.

The following is taken from *Defence and Industry in Cumbria* by Alan Postlethwaite (undated):

'The railways were required to perform heroic endeavours to move unprecedented volumes of fuel, munitions, troops, and casualties. A procession of "Jellicoe Specials", many using the Cumberland coast line to relieve pressure on the main west coast line over Shap, carried huge tonnages of coal to fuel the Northern Fleet through the Scottish ports. Extra capacity was required at Carlisle to cope with the volumes of traffic. Locomotives and wagons were borrowed from the larger railway companies to supplement the limited resources of the local operators. The Kent and Leven viaducts on the Furness line required major reinforcement to handle the heavy traffic. Of all the costs of the war undoubtedly the greatest was the human one of the loss of so many of a generation of young skilled and productive workers.'

The main Carlisle to Maryport line (the Maryport & Carlisle Railway) was completed in 1845. The line between Workington and Cleator Moor was opened in 1879. The line continued from Workington to a junction with the London & North Western Railway (LNWR) at Siddick, two miles north of Workington. Fifty men of the Cleator and Workington Junction Railway joined up and six lost their lives.

No war memorial erected by the Cleator & Workington Junction Railway has been traced. Extensions of the Furness Railway took the railway to Whitehaven in 1865. From the Furness Railway, 515 men joined up and 68 lost their lives.

The Furness Railway's war memorial, unveiled on 16 October 1921, is located at Barrow railway station. Private JS Nixon (died 1917), Argyll and Sutherland Highlanders, 1st/5th Battalion, a fireman for the Furness Railway, lived in Marlborough Street, Whitehaven. Private Harry Shimmin (died 1916, aged 20), son of Mr and Mrs Philip Shimmin of Senhouse Street, Whitehaven, was a number taker for the Furness Railway.

The LNWR's war memorial is located just off Euston Road, in front of Euston railway station in London: 31,744 employees of the company served in the Armed Forces during the war; 3,700 lost their lives. Private Joseph Bulman is commemorated there and was a relief clerk at Whitehaven. He was in the Royal Engineers, 96th Light Railway Operating Company and died in December 1917. Private J Fisher, Border Regiment, 2nd Battalion, was an underman at Parton. He died in March 1916, aged 37 and is buried at Whitehaven Cemetery.

The Joint Committee's (the LNW and Furness Joint Lines) war memorial was originally located on the platform side of the main station building at Moor Row. It is now at the Moor Row Working Men's Club.

Cleator Moor, Parton and Whitehaven lines, 1904.

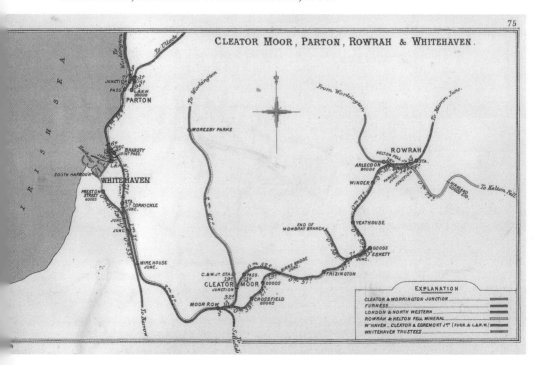

The Conscientious Objectors Memorial atWoodland.

Five men are commemorated: Corporal Thomas Glover (died 1918, aged 23), a clerk at Cleator Moor, was in the 2nd Border. Private George Kitchin (died 1918), a clerk and son of William Henry and Jane of Distington, was with the 1st Border. Private JB Robinson (died 1918, aged 18), a signalman at Cleator Moor, was in the 4th Border and is buried at St Leonard's Churchyard, Cleator. Lance-Corporal (Signaller) John Sewell (died 1916, aged 26), a clerk at Egremont, was in the 2nd Border.

Today the Cumbrian Coast line is the only survivor of a once dense network of railways serving local industries. Stations once included Whitehaven Newtown (closed 1855) and Woodland near Broughton-in-Furness, close to an unusual inscription on a craggy outcrop of rock on Green Moor. It consists of a series of initials, six in all and the name A Boosey. What is most interesting is the short inscription which accompanies them: CON OBJECTORS 1916. It is something of a mystery why the initials of conscientious objectors should be included here, unless it is some attempt to name and shame. Everyone in the area at the time would know who they were.

Chapter Fourteen

Words of War

LIEUTENANT-COLONEL DAN Mason, a solicitor who was educated at St Bees School, joined the Cumberland Volunteer Artillery in 1900 – which was re-formed into the TF in 1908 - and he retired in 1922. He was Mayor of Workington from 1927 to 1929. Some of the most interesting items from his collection of papers are three of his Field Message Books, which span the Cumberland Artillery's part in the campaigns in Gallipoli, in Sinai, and on the Western Front.

In August 1915, the situation at Gallipoli settled into static trench warfare, with occasional patrolling, raiding, bombing and mining. Mason notes that after the end of August they were 'short of ammunition', and describes life thereafter as 'Dull routine with occasional excitement'. Nevertheless, between the beginning of September and the end of December Mason registered fifty-seven targets using 50lb Lyddite and, from the beginning of December, a further forty-three with fused 40lb Shrapnel ammunition.

In his lecture notes, he gives a snapshot of daily life on the gun position:

Life on Gallipoli:
Water bad – food good
Heat, flies & dust & smell Bathing
Later frost & snow & floods
Letters a month old
never sure of dates
Porridge from biscuits
Gallipoli oven
No wood, no sandbags
a primitive communal life
grasshoppers, centipedes, spiders
kestrel hawks & owls
wild geese in Octr
heat made you listless
dysentery amoebic

jaundice with the rain & dust paste.

Mason's description of their final actions on Gallipoli, on 8 January 1916, in his lecture notes, is brief and stark:

burnt wagons

killed horses

barbed wire – flour bags

ham in trenches.

The guns, however, were saved, though without their limbers. In the early hours of 9 January, Mason's two howitzers, together with the two from 1st Battery and thirty-three other guns, were hoisted aboard the freighter *Clan MacRae*. At 3.45, while she was still in sight of the shore, those on board were able to see what Mason describes as the 'final fire', when the mass of abandoned stores and equipment went up in flames.

With his papers is a handwritten 'List of Killed'. The following are from Whitehaven: Bombardier John Edwards (died 1918), aged 31; Gunner Henry Fox (died 15 July 1917), aged 34; Sergeant Hugh McKenzie (died 1918). Fox, husband of Ann Jane Fox of Plumblands Lane, Whitehaven, is buried at Whitehaven Cemetery.

This locally-kept schedule seems, however, to be incomplete, as the 42nd Division History lists additional names. The following are from Whitehaven: Sergeant William Coulthard (died 1915), aged 35; Driver F Signoratti (died 1918), aged 22. The Carlisle Cathedral memorial includes four other names. Coulthard is buried at Whitehaven Cemetery.

The Cumberland Artillery's largest single loss occurred two-and-a-half weeks after the armistice. On 28 November 1918, near Hautmont, eight men of D/210 Battery were killed outright when a wagon loaded with ammunition exploded. Four of them were among those who had mobilised in August 1914.

The static and dull nature of trench warfare and the close proximity of the enemy – which meant that they could be heard, and their breakfast cooking smelled, although rarely seen – caused many men to be curious about the men they were facing. In the Christmas Truce of 1914, they had a chance to meet their opposite numbers, an experience many men found to be profoundly moving.

The following is an extract published in the *Whitehaven News* 18 February 1915:

'Private Dixon, 9100, D Company. Head Quarters Staff, 2nd Border Regiment British Expeditionary Force, writes us:- "Just a line from a few of the Whitehaven lads out at the front. We get your paper sent to us every week, and are very pleased to read the news of the dear old home. There is quite a good number of Whitehaven lads out here, but a few have 'gone under.' Our regiment has had it very tough since they came out. We numbered about 1,300 when we left home, and now there is only about 150 left, and I happen to be one of the lucky ones. I am proud to say our regiment heads the list in our brigade for Distinguished Conduct medals. At Christmas we got quite friendly with the Germans. There was no firing on both sides for about ten days, and we used to go over the trenches and talk to them and exchange souvenirs, but every one we spoke to that could speak English said they wished it was over. I was surprised when one told me he had a wife in Piccadilly and another said he drove a taxi at Fulham. We've started scrapping again; and I can tell you it is not very nice in the trenches up to the knees in water. We do four days in the trenches and then go to billets for four days. We are all quite cheerful and confident of success so we just say the old saying 'What odds, so long as we're happy?' Well I must draw to a close, and wishing your paper every success - We remain, 'A few marrows* fra Whitehaven.'"

(Now spelt marras, it is a Cumbrian word for friends).

Chapter 15

Wartime refugees in Cumberland

THE FIRST MENTION of the Belgian Relief Effort in the *Whitehaven News* is a fund-raising dance at Ravenglass Village Hall on 5 November, 1914 followed the next day by a Ball at Captain Shaw's School, Bootle. In Whitehaven, the first practical mention is on 22 October when there was an appeal to provide furniture, bedding and kitchen utensils to furnish the old Bank of Whitehaven building in Coates Lane as accommodation for around three dozen refugees. This was co-ordinated by the Whitehaven Distress and Relief Committee, who also appealed for money for the around £500 per year estimated costs to maintain these facilities.

There had been an earlier letter on 24 August asking for national donations, from John William Young of Trafalgar Villa, Bransty quoting the Belgian Consul in Edinburgh who had Germans quartered in his father's house in Belgium, his 80-year-old mother being held as prisoner by the Germans and whose wife and children had had to flee from the invasion.

On 29 October, there is a very detailed report about the arrival of the first refugees at Whitehaven. The Whitehaven Colliery Company had paid for their train fares from London and company housing at Kells, and was going to provide work for them at Ladysmith Pit. They arrived on 27 October. They were from Charleroi, and had left Ostend on 18 October with little but their clothes. They were: Madame Pauline Nys and children Marie & Bertha; Adam Theophell; John Isenbough; Joseph Naulaerts; Emile Francken; Joseph van Meerbeck; Jules Vilain Lebon Fortune (youth); Elarts Theophell (youth); and Alphonse Van Vlasel (youth).

On 5 November, we are told that there are already fifty-seven refugees in the Penrith area, ten at Maryport and twenty-nine at Workington, with promises of space for fifty at Alston, thirty at Whitehaven and forty at Keswick with arrangements ongoing at Longtown, Brampton, Cockermouth and Wigton.

On 6 November, St Begh's had a rummage sale for the Mayor's fund for the relief of Belgian refugees, by auction at the Church Street Sale Room.

On 10 November, twenty-one refugees in five families, ranging from babes-in-arms to a lady aged over 80, arrived by the last train to take up the accommodation in the old bank building. On 12 November, we learn that Meadow View, Gosforth had been furnished ready to receive refugees. On 13 November, there was a concert at Harrington to raise funds to furnish a house in Church Road to house two refugee families.

By 12 November, a Monsieur Fosty and family were living at Underwood, Bootle (the home of Mr Hudson of Manchester). They had arrived on 26 October, according to the *Millom Gazette*. One of them worked for Belgian railways and one was a dentist. On 18 November, four refugees arrived at Harrington to the house that had been prepared for them, owned by Mr Blacklock.

On 23 November, six refugees arrived at The Cross, Hensingham by the 2pm train direct from London Euston to Corkickle arriving at 10.15pm where they were met by the Vicar, Reverend CEA Blackburn, who also acted as interpreter. Four of them spoke Flemish, the other two Walloon. They had had a seven-week trip from Cerde, Belgium via Holland, where they were market gardeners.

The Cross had accommodation for many more refugees. These families were Roman Catholic and attended the RC School. By 18 December, more had arrived at The Cross and a man, wife and child were staying with Mrs Moore at Cartgate. The plan was for the men of this second party to work making munitions at Workington.

On 6 December, there was a concert in aid of the Belgian Relief Fund at the Hippodrome, Cleator Moor – the building being provided free of charge by the proprietors Messrs Relph & Pedley. On 12 December, a party of refugees arrived at Herding Nab, Seascale. They were; Joseph van de Pas; his wife Marie, and children Joseph Virginia (aged 14); Pierre (aged six); and Charles (aged 14 months). They were Walloon speakers. On 23 December, two married couples arrived at Foumart Hill, Frizington, the cottage being provided by Mr T Dixon of Rheda. By 8 January 1915, two families had arrived at 41 Main Street, Haverigg from Antwerp. They were joined the next day by Jean Frerard, an engineer from Liege aged 52; his wife Maria, 52; and his daughter Felicie, aged 25; plus Joseph Lecoq, a machine engineer from Vorviers, aged 54.

In mid-January 1915, it was announced that Millom expected to receive between 300 and 500 Belgian refugees, who would work at Barrow Shipyard. The arrangements to accommodate them were made by the Millom Ratepayers' Association. Most of the ex-soldiers among them had been interned at Flushing in Holland and many had been forced to work for the Germans.

By 15 January, Lieutenant Goosens of the Belgian Army was at Woodlands, Bootle. He had been seriously wounded in the leg on 25 October 1914. As at 20 January 1915, the number of refugees in Allerdale above Derwent were: Hensingham, twenty-one; Seascale, seven; Gosforth, three; Frizington, four; and Harrington, eight. Around 21 January, a further family of five 'peasant refugees' were due at Maryport, to a house on Collin's Terrace. A box of toys had been sent for the children of the existing refugees there by Princess Marie Jose of Belgium.

On 27 January, there was a concert for the Refugee fund at the Co-operative Hall given by the Haverigg Madrigal Choir and the Haverigg Minstrel Troupe.

On 28 January, an Anglo-Belgian concert was given at the Drill Hall, Millom.

Throughout that week, a contingent of refugees arrived at Millom daily - about 260 in total in the week. Between two and six were put up by individuals in their homes. A special workmen's train was laid on to Barrow with about 500 seats. However, it was unheated, leading to some of the Belgians moving to Barrow. The number in Millom continued to be supplemented in February by the arrival of wives and children, and a Belgian shop opened, initially just selling Belgian newspapers. On 9 February, Monsieur Alfred Bertrand left Bootle to rejoin the Belgian army in France. His wife and daughter remained.

At Cockermouth, Private Eland of the 5th Borders had met a Belgian sailor called Pyson on the mail boat *Leopold II*. He had been able to put him in touch with his wife, Angele, and child who were living at Derwent Street, Cockermouth. Private Eland survived the war.

On 27 March 1915, a manure cart belonging to Millom Co-op separated from its horse in the centre of Millom due to the shaft breaking. The horse then careered through the town when one of the refugees, Dubosch Heliodore, pluckily managed to stop it. He lived in Albert Street with his wife and son.

On 8 April 1915, there were now 640 men using the workmen's train from Millom to Vickers daily – mainly Belgians – and that there were rumours of another large contingent arriving in Barrow soon, also that Haverigg householders have room for 200 refugees. There was also a meeting of the Belgians at Millom Co-op Hall on 5 April to set up a comforts fund for their own soldiers fighting on the banks of the River Yser; each man to contribute 1s per week to the fund.

By 6 May 1915, some of the Belgians were starting to leave Millom, on the expiry of their three-month contracts to return to the front in France and to make munitions for the war, with the first men leaving on Sunday 2 May. A large contingent remained, though.

On Sunday 30 May 1915, there was a riot at Kells, an area of Whitehaven, between the Belgian and English miners. There had been long-standing simmering resentment amongst some of the locals that some of the refugees were of fighting age, and able to fight, but were instead working at the pits here while many pitmen were away fighting in the British army. The riot started after some intemperate remarks by a group of nine drunk Belgians. A superintendent, two inspectors and five constables were sent to quell the disturbance. The next day, the miners at Ladysmith Pit went on strike, demanding the removal of all the Belgian miners.

By the end of July 1915, a Belgian lady teacher had arrived in Millom, and was teaching at St James' RC School. About seventy new Belgians arrived at this time, bringing the total in the town to over 650. On 9 September, it was reported that there were a number of Belgian soldiers on leave in Millom. That same week, a Belgian was found guilty at Whitehaven of being drunk and disorderly and was fined 13/-. There is an interesting comment in the *Millom Gazette* of 6 August that their uniform has recently changed to khaki.

A sign of the ongoing tensions between the English and Belgian miners in Whitehaven was a court case on 20 September 1915 against a 29-year-old Belgian coalminer of the charge of tub-sticking, the 'crime' of putting your numbered token on other miners' coal tubs in order to claim their work as your own. Tokens with numbers were attached by workers on full tubs of coal. Each working party had a number. When the tub arrived at the pit top, it was checked. Miners were paid on the basis of what they filled, so it would have been regarded as a serious charge. He was acquitted of the charge. More than 300 Belgians lived at Alabaster Buildings, Sandwith. On 4 October 1915, Jean Francois Frenay, aged 50, of Barnes Lane, Workington was killed by a rock-fall while hagging coal at Lowca. He had worked at Millmort Colliery, Belgium before the war.

At the meeting of the Whitehaven Borough Non-Provided Schools Sub-Committee of 18 October, the numbers of Belgian children at each school in the Borough was noted (a total of fifty-two children): St Begh's, sixteen; St Gregory & St Patrick, six; Crosthwaite Mixed, two; Earl of Lonsdale's (Monkwray) Mixed, twelve; Earl of Lonsdale's (Monkwray) Infants, eleven; Trinity Mixed, three; Trinity Infants, one; Council Infants, one.

On Saturday 13 November, the Belgian Society of Millom gave a Grand Concert, for comforts for serving Belgian soldiers. Notable at this event was the appearance of Sergeant Bughin of the 13th Regiment of the Belgian Army. He wore the medals Chevalier Leopold d'Or and the Croix de Guerre. During November, 73 Belgian soldiers visited Millom for a three or four day holiday – each was presented with 5/- (£25 today) pocket money by the local refugee community.

Throughout their stay, there were cases of drunk and disorderly brought against the Belgians, but no more or less than among the general population. There were also regular cases of failing to register a change of address with the police. On a happier note there were regular concerts given by the Belgians, most of which also attracted the general populace, and all were a great success. Many aimed to raise funds either for Belgian soldiers' comforts or for displaced Belgians in Holland.

One of these concerts was on 3 January 1916, with music provided by the Millom Lyric Orchestra and dancing from 9.15pm until 4am next morning. All proceeds from that concert were to assist Belgian families who suffered in consequence of the Powder Factory catastrophe at Graville St Honorine, Le Havre. In January 1916, a few of the Millom Belgians emigrated to the Belgian Congo where they had found work.

On Saturday 15 July, a concert, wrestling competition, sports and dance were held in the field opposite the Station Hotel, Millom, organised by the Millom Anglo-Belgian Society to aid and feed Belgian orphans being starved by the Germans in their own land.

Within documents held at Cumbria Record Office, there are a number of letters relating to the marriage at Prestwich, Manchester in the June quarter of 1916 of Harry Morgenstern (a Jew from Palestine working in Whitehaven) to Leah Auerbach from Russia. After marriage they are known to have gone to live at Barrow and had two children, Sarah and Abraham.

On 28 August 1916, a Belgian miner, Theophile Wustenberg, residing at Northside, Workington, was killed by a rock fall at Lowca Pit. He was married with three children. On 8 September, a German living at Millom died under unexplained circumstances at the Redhills Quarry, Millom where he worked. He was Charles Clark, aged 53. He was of German nationality and had come to Millom in autumn 1914. On June 28 1915, he was arrested and interned but was liberated and returned to Millom after a short time.

During January 1917, some Flemish Belgian soldiers came on holiday to Millom. And by that date, there are also a few Dutch residents in

Millom. At Christmas 1916, the school children of Millom raised £13/5/- (today's equivalent would be £1,300) at their own Christmas lunch in aid of the 'starving little Belgians'.

On 11 January 1917, a Mrs Arends of Arlecdon became chargeable to Whitehaven Poor Law Union. She was the wife of a German sailor interned at Knockaloe on the Isle of Man, Edward Christopher Arends.

From the *Millom Gazette* of 8 June 1917, we learn that Millom had a Belgian football club, Le Union de Belge FC and on the 15 June, we learn of the success of 'The Little Belgian' of Millom (his real name is not given) in the Ji-Jitsu v English Boxing match at Whitehaven. It raised £57 (£5,750) which he distributed among the poor of Whitehaven.

In the summer of 1918, Mary Farish Brown (1875-1940) of Lowther Street, Whitehaven, daughter of the solicitor Thomas Brown, was awarded the Gold Medaille de la Reine Elizabeth for her assistance to the refugees during the war. This is one of three such medals currently known in the county – the others being at Carlisle and Kendal. In August, the refugees at the Old Bank gave her a coffee service in gratitude with an arrangement of flowers in the Belgian national colours from the children.

On 29 October 1918, Michael – a child aged four years six months of Michael Leclerq of Bardy Lane, Whitehaven – died of scalding from falling into a bath of hot water which had been prepared for his father. He is buried at Whitehaven Cemetery. The family had lost another child, Marielle Ferdinand aged four months, in March 1916 when they were living at the Alabaster Works (cause of death unknown), Wetheral parish, Cumberland.

On 22 December 1918, in view of the impending departure of the first of the refugees, a Thanksgiving Concert was held at Millom Recreation Hall. On Friday 17 January 1919, the first twenty left Millom for home, and another thirty on 20 January. Their departure was a hugely emotional occasion for both Belgians and English. Only about a dozen now remained in Millom.

On 2 February, a special train departed at 10.15am from Bransty station to Newcastle for Antwerp conveying around 200 refugees. Monsieur & Madame Cloempoel presented Mr HC Reynalds, secretary of Whitehaven Colliery Company, with a silver mounted walking stick and companion set of pipes in grateful appreciation of the Belgian miners for all that the Company had done for them. The platform was crowded with people, who gave the Belgians a very hearty send off as the train streamed out and fog signals on the line were exploded.

This chapter has ended up concentrating on the Millom story, rather than the original intent of Whitehaven. This is because the Millom population was by far the largest and also the story is far more comprehensively told in the *Millom Gazette* than in the *Whitehaven News*. It also seems to be true that the Millom model of housing the people in the town in small numbers per house led to much better integration than the Whitehaven model of housing them all together at a remote location outside Sandwith. It was also helped by the fact that at Millom the refugees were engaged in work which clearly helped the war effort, rather than at Whitehaven where they were working in the pits – although this was just as essential in its own way to the war, especially as so many local pitmen had volunteered for war service, but there was an undercurrent that the refugees had taken locals' jobs.

On 23 March 1919, a further party of Whitehaven refugees were to leave Newcastle by ship for Belgium. They actually departed Whitehaven and were the last of the families who had been living at the Old Bank since 29 November 1914: Monsieur and Madame Callut plus four children, Monsieur and Madame Van Den Boegarde and Madame Michel. They had lived at Mericourt and left on a French steamer. That was torpedoed and the passengers rescued by a passing English vessel. Both men were miners in Whitehaven. Mericourt village no longer exists so the families are to return to Tourcoing. Also leaving that day from this area were Monsieur and Madame Steart and three children.

A formal letter of thanks for the hospitality of the United Kingdom to the refugees was sent in August 1919 from His Excellency Monsieur le Baron de Brocqueville, Minister of the Interior for Belgium.

An interviewee for June Thistlethwaite's *Cumbrian Women Remembered* (1995) said that during the First World War there were three Belgian evacuees at Allonby School.

> 'They wore black smocks, not like our clothes, and we sort of made fun of them at first but we got used to these kiddies and accepted them as ordinary people. About this time, there were some disabled soldiers at Allonby living in a big house with a verandah, which must have been a convalescent home.'

Disabled, by war poet Wilfred Owen (1893-1918), explores the effects of war on those who live through it by comparing the present life of an injured soldier to his past hopes and accomplishments. The women he joined up to impress are ignoring him: his courage means nothing to them now he's in a wheelchair. Attitudes had to change; they were war heroes who had sacrificed their bodies for the nation. Private Robert

Adair, Cheshire Regiment, of Whitehaven had his right leg amputated. The *Whitehaven News* reported on 10 May 1917 that Private Coward's foot had been blown off and that he was in hospital in France. He was from Silecroft. Private Francis Coan, 2nd Border, from Whitehaven fought in the First World War and lost his arm.

In August 1916, a floral fete was held in Millom for the town's disabled soldiers and sailors. It raised £51 (equivalent to £4,500) to aid those who, following the war, could not continue in their usual employment. And in October 1916, a Whitehaven War Pensions Local Committee meeting was held at Town Hall to deal with discharged soldiers and disabled officers and men. In April 1917, a Bransty Station flag day, Whitehaven was held in aid of war disabled former employees. In July 1917, there was a garden fete in Beckermet in aid of the Whitehaven & District Blinded Soldiers' and Sailors' Fund. The Royal British Legion created the Poppy Appeal to help those returning from the First World War. It is still helping today's Armed Forces' families in much the same way, whether coping with bereavement, living with disability, or finding employment.

Chapter 16

The Yellow Earl

HUGH CECIL LOWTHER, 5th Earl of Lonsdale (1857-1944) – or Lord Lonsdale – was an English nobleman, sportsman and explorer. Lord Lonsdale, who was sent to Eton, where he lasted a year, and then to a Swiss finishing school, inherited enormous wealth from the West Cumberland coalmines and had residences at Lowther Castle near Penrith, Westmorland (designated a castle between 1806 and 1814); Whitehaven Castle, Barleythorpe; and Carlton Terrace, London. He held office as Mayor of Whitehaven in 1894-6.

Portrait of Lord Lonsdale (1930) by Sir John Lavery.

He was called the Yellow Earl because his family colours were yellow and it was his favourite colour. He founded the AA – hence the old colours for the AA. Also, Westmorland Conservatives have always used yellow as their party colours instead of the traditional blue, which naturally has caused confusion with the Liberal party colours. He, otherwise known as 'Lordy', founded the Boxing Club and, later in his life, he presented the Lonsdale belts for championship boxing.

Whitehaven Castle, c 1906: Whitehaven Castle was still Lowther-owned in 1906 and was a walled estate. *(Ralph Lewthwaite)*

Kaiser Wilhelm II (1859-1941) had a close relationship before the war with Lord Lonsdale and, according to ES Turner's *Dear Old Blighty* (Faber & Faber, 2012) about life on the home front, the bust of the Emperor retained its place of honour at Lowther Castle. For one of the Kaiser's visits, the *Raven* on Ullswater, which still sails Ullswater today, had her decks painted yellow and was used as a Royal Yacht.

Lord Lonsdale's great nephew, Jim Lowther, said Hugh Lonsdale and the Kaiser had a shared love of country sports and sailing, as well as having birthdays that were very close together (the Kaiser described Lord Lonsdale as his celestial twin). The friendship burgeoned and it resulted eventually in a visit to Lowther Castle in 1895 by the Kaiser for some grouse shooting. The Kaiser arrived on the east coast and travelled to Penrith by train where he was welcomed by the whole town of Penrith. He proceeded to travel to Lowther Castle, where he spent a week.

Author, farmer and landowner Beatrix Potter (1866–1943), who campaigned against the conscription of working farm horses, watched the procession and recorded the following entry in her diary:

'Tuesday August 15 1895. We consumed three whole hours waiting to see the Emperor, not very well worth it. I had seen him in London. I think he is stouter. I was not particularly excited. I think it is disgraceful to drive fine horses like that. First came a messenger riding a good roan belonging to Bowness, which we could hear snorting before they came in sight, man and horse both dead-beat. He reported the Emperor would be up in ten minutes, but it was twenty.

The procession consisted of a mounted policeman with a drawn sword in a state approaching apoplexy, the red coats of the Quorn Hunt, four or five of Lord Lonsdale's carriages, several hires and spare horses straggling after them. There were two horses with an outside rider to each carriage, splendid chestnut thoroughbreds floundering along and clinking their shoes.

They were not going fast when we saw them, having come all the way from Patterdale without even stopping at Kirkstone to water the horses, to the indignation of mine host, and an assembly of three or four hundred who had reckoned on this act of mercy. I think his majesty deserved an accident and rather wonder he didn't have one considering the smallness of the little Tiger sitting on the box to work the break.

The liveries were blue and yellow and the carriages much yellow singularly ugly low tub. With a leather top to shut up sideways. The Emperor, Lord Lonsdale and two ladies in the first, Lady Dudley etc in the second.

'There was a considerable crowd and very small flags. German ones bad to get at short notice, but plenty of tricolours. Lord Lonsdale is red headed and has a harum-scarum reputation, but according to Mr Edmondson, less "stupid" than his predecessor whom he had seen "Beastly droonk" in the road on a Sunday morning.'

The Kaiser, who had a crippled left arm (Erb's palsy), was invited to take a walk at Lowther Castle and shoot a few rabbits. Prior to this, hundreds of rabbits had been caught and caged in a wood and, at a given signal, they were released and the Kaiser bagged 67 rabbits in half an hour.

And then Lord Lonsdale went to visit the Kaiser in Germany a few times. The kings of Italy and Portugal later came to stay at Lowther Castle, and the Kaiser a second time in 1902. The following is taken from *The Advertiser*, Adelaide, South Australia November 17 1902:

'The German Emperor has conferred upon the Earl of Lonsdale a knighthood of the first class of the Order of the Prussian Crown. It was through Lord Lonsdale's instrumentality that a better feeling between Germany and England was brought about after the Kaiser's attempted intervention in connection with the Jameson raid (December 1895 to January 1896) a botched attack   on Paul Kruger's Transvaal Republic, South Africa, carried out by British colonial statesman Leander Starr Jameson and his Company of mercenaries and Bechuanaland policemen. It was intended to trigger an uprising by the primarily British expatriate workers. The raid was ineffective and no uprising took place.'

Lord Lonsdale was Master of the Cottesmore Hunt, which hunts mostly in Rutland, and made great contributions to carry the hunt through the First World War and in its aftermath to ensure the survival of foxhunting. Indeed in his own words to justify his efforts, he stated 'What on earth are officers home from the front going to do with their time if there is no foxhunting for them?' After the war, he became more involved with race horses and became a senior steward of the Jockey Club.

The family fortune was undermined by the extravagance of Lord Lonsdale. The story goes that when he was told he could no longer afford to live at Lowther Castle in the 1940s, he simply just left one night in his Rolls Royce (yellow of course!). He and his wife, Grace, lived in retirement at Barleythorpe, where Grace died in 1942 and Lord Lonsdale

Lowther Castle from postcard dated 1904.

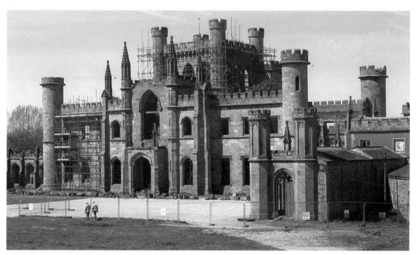

The once spectacular castle is now a derelict shell but a project aims to restore the site to its former glory. *(www.tripadvisor.com)*

in 1944, both being brought back to Lowther for burial.

Lowther Castle was closed in 1937. It was used as an armoured base in the Second World War, including trials for tanks fitted with high powered searchlights designed to blind the enemy. The military concrete roads still lace across the estate fields. The castle's contents were removed in the late 1940s and the roof was removed in 1957. The shell of the castle is still owned by the Lowther Estate Trust.

The Lonsdale Cemetery by Authuille Wood, north of Albert now contains 1,542 Commonwealth burials and commemorations of the First World War. Some 816 of the burials are unidentified but there are special memorials to twenty-two casualties known or believed to be buried among them.

John Joseph Errington, 11th Border, is on the Lonsdale Roll of

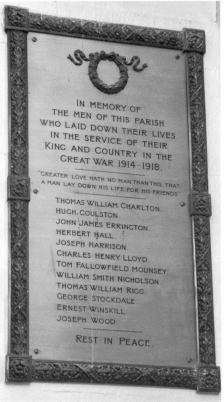

IN MEMORY OF
THE MEN OF THIS PARISH
WHO LAID DOWN THEIR LIVES
IN THE SERVICE OF THEIR
KING AND COUNTRY IN THE
GREAT WAR 1914-1918.

GREATER LOVE HATH NO MAN THAN THIS. THAT.
A MAN LAY DOWN HIS LIFE FOR HIS FRIENDS

THOMAS WILLIAM CHARLTON.
HUGH. COULSTON.
JOHN JAMES ERRINGTON
HERBERT HALL.
JOSEPH HARRISON.
CHARLES HENRY LLOYD
TOM FALLOWFIELD MOUNSEY.
WILLIAM SMITH NICHOLSON
THOMAS WILLIAM RIGG.
GEORGE STOCKDALE
ERNEST WINSKILL.
JOSEPH WOOD

REST IN PEACE.

St Michael's church, Lowther. St Michael's Church is the estate church within the Lowther Castle grounds. It is also known as Lowther Church. *(www.visitcumbria.com.)*

Brass on wooden backboard: This plaque is inside St Michael's church, Lowther. *(Ian Stuart Nicholson).*

Honour and was a gardener at Lowther Hall. He died on 1 July 1916 and is buried at Lonsdale Cemetery. Many more Lonsdales have their names carved on the Thiepval memorial to the missing that dominates the area of the Somme.

Lonsdale Cemetery: Visitors are advised that access to the cemetery is difficult especially in wet weather. *(Commonwealth War Graves Commission).*

Gravestone of JJ Errington, the Lowther Hall gardener.

Chapter 17

Women behind the military

WITHOUT MODERN APPLIANCES, the household routine filled each week and it really did seem like a woman's work was never done. Spring cleaning was a chore which seemed to come around all too soon, and even day to day housework involved a great deal of physical effort and drudgery. Mothers had one day when they baked for the whole week: bread, pastry and pies. And it was a terrible thing if a woman went into a pub. It was 'Eee, his wife goes to pubs, you know.'

The story of the Great War tends to be a story about men. It takes a great deal of effort to see past them to the women, who went into what had been exclusively male areas of employment. It's also far harder to find the women's memorials.

The origins of the Women's Land Army (WLA) lie in the First World War. German naval blockades had successfully impacted on Britain's food imports and there was an acute shortage of farm labour as workers were needed for military service. By 1918, there were 23,000 Land Girls. When the Second World War names were added to the Eskdale Valley Memorial and the memorial rededicated on 10 April 1949,

VAD poster showing uniform.

it was unveiled by Mr James D Porter who had lost a daughter, Ellie, in the Land Army in the First World War.

Ellie Porter, whose name is on the east face of the memorial, died in an accident at Henhull Hall training farm, Nantwich, Cheshire on 4 February 1918, aged 19. Her parents brought her body home on the last train to Ravenglass on 6 February, arriving at midnight. The funeral was at St Catherine's Church, Boot at 2.30pm on 7 February attended by the teachers and children from the Low School. The coffin was borne on

Dress 9325
Transfer 2355

Dress 9325
Transfer 2355

Blouse 9132
Skirt 9339
Transfer 10473

Dress 9321
Transfer 2355

MANAGED WITH COSTUMES LIKE THESE
STYLES IN COATS AND FROCKS

**Styles in coats and frocks:
Women needed the right clothes
for the job. From the luxurious
silks of High Society, to the boots
and breeches of the WLA.**
(Great War Forum)

Mr Russell Parker's cart and Mrs Rea of Gatehouse, Eskdale provided her car for the family. Two of the Land Army girls working at Santon Bridge attended.

Women did not go underground in the Cumberland mines, although they had long been employed on the surface as 'screen lasses' (picking metal and stone out from the coal). But they worked for the Whitehaven Fire Brick and Sewage Pipe Company in place of men during the First World War. This was on Low Road, out towards the cemetery.

Isabella Thompson (1889-1978) of 26 Tangier Street, Whitehaven signed a temporary 'Contract of Trained Nurses employed in Military Hospitals' with the Army Medical Department in October 1915, with her pay and allowances being at the same rates as those paid to members of Queen Alexandra's Imperial Military Nursing Service (QAIMNS), and was a staff nurse, register number 2 Reserve 7883, at Pavilion Military Hospital, Brighton. She renewed her contract 'for 12 months or until my services are no longer required, whichever shall first happen' in October 1917, and resigned from QAIMNS as a staff nurse at Brighton in 1919. During the First World War, this hospital was turned into a specialist unit for Indian servicemen wounded while fighting for British forces.

Her form of application dated 21 September 1915 details the following. She was trained at the Central London Sick Asylum for three years from 1911 until May 1914 as a theatre sister, and left in August 1914. She worked at the War Hospital, Antwerp, Belgium from September 1914 to October 1914 as a theatre sister. She then worked at a war hospital in France. Here, her work is listed as 'Surgical Work in Wards. Also Rheumatic Fever, Pneumonia, Tetanus and Frostbite,

**Doing more than cleaning the house: First World War women workers
at the brickworks.**

November 5th 1914 to February 10th 1915'.

She worked at Camp Hospital, Serbia doing surgical work in wards from April 1915 to July 1915. According to the *Whitehaven News* 27 August 1914, Belle Thompson volunteered for Red Cross work in Belgium. She was awarded a Serb Samaritan Cross and a Serb Red Cross Society Medal, Silver

She lost three brothers in the war. George Gordon Thompson died on 1 March 1917 after being wounded five times; he is commemorated on the Presbyterian and St James' memorials in Whitehaven. Frank Thompson died on 14 April 1917, and Wallace Thompson died on 21 August 1915 – they are both on the St James' memorial. She also had a sister, Laura who became a nurse, like her.

On 10 January 1921, she married Thomas Crook at Christ Church, Whitehaven. She died at Pow Beck Nursing Home, Whitehaven in November 1978 and was buried at Whitehaven Cemetery on 11 November 1978 alongside her husband (who died on 2 March 1961 when they lived at 7 South View Road, Whitehaven). They appear to have had only one child, George Thompson Crook.

Constance Lillian Louise Highton (1898-1918), educated at Calder Girls School, Seascale, was a VAD nurse in the war and died, aged 20, in late 1918 in London. The Highton Window at St John's Church, Keswick – also known as the Resurrection Window – commemorates her.

His Majesty's Factory, Gretna near Carlisle (construction work on the factory started in November 1915) produced cordite – the propellant for shells – for the British army. By 1917, the largest proportion of the workforce were women: 11,576 women to 5,066 men.

It is not entirely clear where the Workington National Shell Factory, which opened in August 1916, was located. According to an article in the *Times and Star* dated 16 November 2012, it was in Havelock Street at a site that was the Workington Toy Factory. However, according to another reference, a list of National Factories Controlled by the Ministry of Munitions, 1915-1918 compiled by Birmingham University, it was in Stanley Street. It was a national projectile factory controlled by the Ministry of Munitions and Miss James was a forewoman at the shell factory, a foretaste perhaps of things to come.

The East Cumberland Shell Factory in Carlisle, set up from scratch in five months as a response to the 'shell crisis' in 1915, was at the Drill Hall in Strand Road. It had a largely female workforce. I have

**Whitehaven Ladies 1917. Their names can be found on
www.donmouth.co.uk**

been unable to establish whether Whitehaven women worked at these
munitions factories. Cumberland Motor Services had to cut back
services in the First World War – this may have been because of a lack
of staff. Thus it seems unlikely that they ran extra works services, and
similarly unlikely that female staff were employed instead.
Presumably, therefore, any extra travelling to work was by railway.

It wasn't all work. A football match between the Workington
Munition Girls and the Carlisle Munition Girls seems to have inspired
the formation of Whitehaven Ladies FC. The team differed from the
others in that it was not munition girls, but schoolteachers which made
up the bulk of their members. They played in skirts, unlike their
counterparts in north-east England who had quickly adopted 'normal'
football attire.

On 5 May 1917, they played the Workington Munition Girls on the
cricket field at Whitehaven to raise funds for the new military hospital

Workington Women Munitions Workers Football Team. *(Visit Scotland).*

at Moresby House. (The Burnyeats donated Moresby House). The game was a financial success: a crowd of around 5,000 were in attendance, and the gross takings were £94 17s 8d. After deduction of expenses, the sum of £89 19s 7d (£6,800 today) was donated to the hospital. As a footballing spectacle it was less of a success - no goals were scored.

The replay took place at Lonsdale Park, Workington on the following Saturday. Four charities were to benefit from the game: the Cumberland PoW Fund; the Workington Red Cross the Workington Star 'Smokes' Fund; and the Bankfield Military Hospital, Workington (the building was demolished in 1985). The Whitehaven team (1-0) scored midway through the first half.

Whitehaven entertained Cockermouth on 16 June 1917, in a match for the benefit of the Mayoress's Relief Fund and the Cockermouth Soldiers' Comforts Fund. A large crowd at the Cricket Field saw Whitehaven win the game 3-1, thanks to a hat-trick from Elsie Wilson, a teacher.

Women made up the larger part of the teams which kept the hospitals open during the war. The Red Cross lists auxiliary hospitals in Britain during the First World War. They include Moresby House Hospital, Whitehaven (later the privately-owned Howgate Hotel and now the Premier Inn); Holmrook Hall (now demolished); and Hazelbank, Gosforth. Auxiliary hospitals were attached to central military hospitals, which looked after patients who remained under military control. Fusehill Workhouse in Carlisle was converted to a military hospital 'for 500 wounded soldiers in the area' and opened on 16 October 1917.

Moresby House was donated as the hospital by Sarah Burnyeat, the mother of William John Dalzell Burnyeat (d 1916) who was chairman of the Whitehaven Rural Tribunal until his resignation due to ill health on 28 March 1916. His parents lived at the nearby Millgrove in Moresby; they could afford to donate Moresby House.

The patients at these auxiliary hospitals were generally less seriously wounded than at other hospitals and they needed to convalesce. The servicemen preferred the auxiliary hospitals to military hospitals because they were not so strict, they were less crowded and the surroundings were more homely.

There are seventeen names of staff and volunteers of all types for Hazelbank, including the doctor and the vicar – the rest are all women, some VADs, according to *The War Work of Auxiliary Hospitals and Voluntary Aid Detachments of Cumberland, Westmoreland and Part of North West Lancashire* by George Hermon Griffin.

During the Second World War, Holmrook Hall was requisitioned by the Admiralty on behalf of the Royal Navy, with locals told that it was a rest home for shipwrecked and distressed soldiers. In fact, strategically located between Royal Ordnance Factory (ROF) Drigg and ROF Sellafield, it was the Royal Navy bomb and munitions training school between 1943 and 1946, under the title HMS *Volcano*.

Midwife Clara Benn, a British civilian nurse during the First World War, spoke to Radio Cumbria in 1984, at the age of 85. She worked in a hospital at Cleator Moor, likely to be Galemire Hospital. Civilian patients came to her hospital. It was sheer hard work getting the patients better, she said. When asked about hygiene, she said that there were a lot of injections and that there was pneumonia but no penicillin. She said: 'Used to get up at 6.30am, on wards at 7am. Up to 8.30pm with two hours relief in the afternoon or evening. Had half days on alternate Sundays. Wages were £10 a year. For the first three months, we had to buy our own uniform. Later during the war, we got a war bonus: £15 the first year, £18 the second year and £20 the third year.'

Chapter Eighteen

Those at home are thinking of us

DOMESTIC TASKS SUCH as sewing and knitting took on a military cast. Under the direction of the St Bees Village Ladies Committee, the village produced day-shirts and nightshirts and helpless case shirts and socks, mittens and stockings. They sent them to the Red Cross and to the Norfolk Military Hospital and to Lord Kitchener's Appeal (for 100,000 men to join the Army, 1914). The *Whitehaven News* 24 September 1914 reported on the success of the Queen Mary's Needle-work Guild in Cleator Moor. It had so far collected 300 garments and £25 (£2,500 today).

The same newspaper on 7 January 1915 includes a letter from Private WJ Shaw, 5th Border Regiment, a Corney soldier at the front. It was a letter to his parents, of High Kinmont, Corney, Bootle, stating that he was having a very rough time, the weather being very severe, but the presents received from unknown donors from Bootle were greatly appreciated. There is no trace of Private Shaw in the CWGC records, nor mention of his dying in the *Whitehaven News* and *Millom Gazette*, so the evidence suggests that he survived the war. There is no memorial at Corney and he is not on Waberthwaite or Bootle memorials that between them appear to cover Corney.

The *Whitehaven News* of 3 August 1916 prints a letter of thanks received by Miss Berwick of Maudsyke, Drigg:

'Dear Miss Berwick, I take upon myself the privilege of writing to thank you for the gift of socks bearing a note from yourself. It has fallen to my lot to issue to my company the result of your efforts, and I am voicing the feeling of the recipients in tendering you our sincerest thanks. We are all looking forward to the day when many (if not all) will return to dear Old England having accomplished that which we set out to do. Yours sincerely, Harry C Larkin, 1/12 Loyal North Lane, Regiment (Pioneers), B.E.F. 22nd July 1916'.

A letter in the *Whitehaven News* 13 August 1914 from the Cleator Moor Boys Scouts Bandage Brigade asked readers for gifts of rolls of common unbleached calico or the money to buy the same in order for the Boy Scouts to make thousands of bandages for the wounded of all nations. And various

Scout leaders, such as CJJ Harris, were required to relinquish their appointments and set off to serve in the Forces. The paper of 17 September 1914 says that he has left Whitehaven for Chester to join the Royal Garrison Artillery and that he was seen off by large numbers of Scouts.

In August 1914, the Seascale Golf Club held an Open Mixed Foursome Medal Competition. Entry was 2s 6d to benefit the War Relief Fund. In January 1915, Miss Nancy Jackson of Sella Park, Calderbridge, made an appeal for the Blue Cross Society to aid the work among the wounded and suffering horses at the front. The sum of £35 (£3,500) had been sent to the Society so far. In February 1915, the Frizington Cigarette Fund Committee sent parcels of cigarettes and woollens to troops. In April 1915, the total number of eggs brought or sent to the Egremont depot for the week ending 25 April 1915 totalled 1,946. They were despatched to the central depot in London for the troops. The *Whitehaven News* 22 July 1915 reports on a request in Whitehaven for socks for the 2nd Border Regiment and old razors for the troops. In Egremont in August 1915, a hound trailing event was held in aid of the 5th Border Regiment in France to raise funds to buy tobacco and in December 1915, a maiden hound trail was held in aid of hospital beds. In Whitehaven on 2 December 1915, there was an agricultural jumble sale in aid of British Farmers' Red Cross Fund.

In December 1915, the Whitehaven British Women's Temperance Association held a concert for wives and mothers of soldiers and sailors. The temperance movement – which advocated teetotalism – received an unexpected boost due to state intervention when the Liberal government passed the Defence of the Realm Act in 1914 at the beginning of the First World War. According to the provisions of this act, pub hours were licensed, beer was watered down and was subject to a penny a pint extra tax.

A rummage sale at Seascale in November 1916 raised £37 (£3,300) for the parish soldiers' Christmas presents.

Chapter 19

Two PoW camps, and Cumberland PoWs in Germany

DURING THE FIRST World War, there was one Prisoner of War (PoW) camp which was variously called by the following four names: Lamplugh/Rowrah/Arlecdon/Salter. It was a satellite of Leigh in Lancashire, a PoW camp located within a mill. It consisted of rows of wooden huts with associated gardens, and many of its PoWs were engaged in farming or forestry. The approximate OS Grid Reference for the camp is NY 063 178. If you find Lamplugh School on Google Maps, there is a small path called 'Sheriff's Gate' which goes towards the cycleway (old Rowrah & Kelton Fell Mineral Railway which closed in 1927) and Salter. Go down this lane towards Salter. The second and third fields on the right-hand side are the fields where I believe the PoW camp was located. On the other side of Sheriff's Gate are a couple of the old quarries.

In July 1917, the *Carlisle Journal* carried a feature under the headline 'Employment of German PoWs'. This stated that the county highways committee had asked Arlecdon and Frizington councils to 'apply to the government for the use of PoWs in improving the approaches to Rowrah Bridge'. The *Journal* reported in March 1918 that '130 Germans were taken back to Rowrah after a day's work'. The *West Cumberland Times* reported on 30 January 1918 on German PoWs on the land, stating '6,000 have been employed on the land for some time past and that they worked in gangs of four or five under the supervision of an English soldier and policeman ploughman, the latter acting as gang foreman.

All the PoWs who died at the Rowrah camp are now buried at the German War Cemetery at Cannock Chase, Staffordshire (Block 14). One, Vinscent Suchanak aged 29, was accidentally killed working in a quarry on 5 May 1917 and was initially buried in the churchyard of St Joseph's, Frizington. He had only worked in the quarry for a few days. According to the inquest report in the *Whitehaven News* on 10 May 1917, he had been transferred from Leigh on 7 November 1916 and originally came from Proboshowitz, Silesia, Germany. There were

Wasdale Head is a small agricultural hamlet.

another ten who died as a result of influenza (November/December 1918); seven were first buried in the churchyard at Lamplugh and the others in St Joseph's, Frizington. The determining factor for the place of burial at that time would have been their religion. One good thing about their re-interment at Cannock Chase is they were buried in adjacent graves regardless of whether they were Protestants or Catholics.

The agreement about these graves being transferred to the new German War Graves Cemetery at Cannock Chase was made in 1959. I believe the Lamplugh/Frizington ones were transferred in 1961 but I do not have an exact date. The transfer of the grave of Fritz Reich from Whitehaven Cemetery would have been about the same time. Cannock Chase was officially opened in 1967 by the President of the Volksbund Deutsche Kriegsgräberfürsorge, the German equivalent of the Commonwealth War Graves Commission. The seven German PoWs who were initially buried at Lamplugh were as follows: Wilhelm Georg Fritz Wengel (died 1918); Emil Richard Fritz Blanke (died 1918); Heinrich Hellweg (died 1918); Adolf Heuer (died 1918); Karl Otto Pretzsch (died 1918); Fritz Timm (died 1918); and Adolf Gustav

Schomann (died 1918). They were all soldiers in the German army.

Wasdale Head PoW camp opened on 1 January 1919 and was a branch of Lamplugh/Rowrah/Arlecdon/Salter (HQ). The Swiss Legation (Carleton House Terrace, London SW1) visited Wasdale Head PoW camp on 19 June 1919. The report was as follows:

'There are at present 36 German military PoWs at this camp. Wasdale Head is a deep and romantic hollow surrounded by lofty mountains, and situated about one mile from Wast Water Lake. The scenery around is wild and inspiring. The east side of Wasdale valley is bounded by the huge Scafell or Scowfell Group including Scafell Pike (3,210ft.) the highest mountain in England.

Wasdale Head camp can be reached by motor car from Seascale station on the Furness Railway.

The camp occupies the premises of one old farm house at a short distance from Wast Water Hotel, a favourite centre for numerous excursions. One is quite surprised to find a prisoner of war camp in this part of the country, known as the English Lake District.

There is not a yard of barbed wire about the place to spoil the effect of the beautiful and peaceful scenery.

The large farm house though roughly constructed with stones from the river and mortar is wind and weatherproof and spacious enough to afford ample accommodation for the prisoners and the British Guard.

Three dormitories have been set apart and fitted out with the usual accommodations with the addition of small comforts improvised by the inmates of the camp.

At present the stream close by serves as ablution place and a large sized bath built of cement by the prisoners in a room adjacent to the kitchen provides the comfort of a weekly hot bath. A dining and recreation room exists but is not required at this time of the year. The kitchen and storerooms are well appointed and convenient. All perishable foodstuffs arrive at the camp three times a week other stores once a week.

There is no regular medical service, the nearest doctor lives about 20 miles from Wasdale Head and can only be available in case of an emergency.

A German interpreter, a son of the Bavarian Mountains quickly set our mind at ease when he told us that in his native place there was no doctor for miles and miles and that no-one was ever ill. He did not say this with the meaning of post hoc ergo proper hoc, but spoke with the confidence of a man who has never known a day's illness. Wasdale Head camp evidently also enjoys this double immunity from disease and a doctor.

The prisoners are employed in river work making a new bed for the river Irt. They work for 54 hours per week weather permitting, and are paid the rate of 1?d per hour.

General conditions. We spent quite a long time inspecting this camp talking with the prisoners in camp and watching them while at work. Their outward appearance speaks for their well being and the few complaints which were received were of no importance.

We left the camp with the parting wish that this wonderful mountain valley might soon by freed from the presence of the prisoners of war camp and the inmates returned to peaceful work in their own country.'

An example of a PoW in Germany is Corporal James Carr. A letter to his wife appears in the *Whitehaven News* 6 May 1915. He had previously been reported killed. Meanwhile, an account by Ms Flynn of Duke Street, Whitehaven of her experiences in Germany appears in the edition of 29 October 1914. She was a local amateur operatic performer detained as 'prisoner of war' by the family she lived with in Germany before being sent home.

Corporal Stanley Hall of Settle Street, Millom was taken PoW on 28 August 1914. He returned to the UK in February 1916, initially to hospital but back home to Millom on or around 17 March 1916. He died at home on 24 March 1916 and was buried at Millom Holy Trinity Church on 27 March 1916.

Chapter 20

ARMISTICE and PEACE

AT ABOUT 11.30 on the morning of 11 November 1918, a rocket was fired at Whitehaven (the shipwreck signal) yet on this fine clear day there was no sign of a ship ashore.

Then the town fire alarm siren was sounded continuously, but there was no fire.

Then a second rocket was fired.

Then the only ship in harbour blew its horn with all its might, yet it was not in distress.

Why, what was afoot?

And then the bells of St Nicholas' Church on Lowther Street in the heart of the town began to ring.

Such was the beginning of the great celebrations in Whitehaven of the signing of the Armistice which was formally announced by Mr McGowan, Chairman of the Magistrates sitting at the Court, the news having come by telephone, from south and east and west.

There was then a rush for flags, for streamers, for bunting. The shops of the town all closed for the day and all the school-children were liberated from attendance at school (they were granted the whole week off). The streets became thronged.

A meeting of the Town Council was hastily summoned and it was decided to hold a great united Public Thanksgiving Service at St Nicholas' Church. There was a march round the town of wounded soldiers and others, addressed by the Mayor 'amid scenes of great enthusiasm', far greater than those on the Jubilee Days of Queen Victoria.

Late in the evening the bellman went round the town announcing the Thanksgiving Service for 3pm the next day with all shops to close again for that afternoon.

Tuesday 12 dawned a fine bright day, following the first keen frost of the season.

Never in this town was there so great a gathering as for this service, which began with a procession of the Mayor and Corporation from the Town Hall. The service was attended by the Clergy of all the denominations. The Sermon was preached by the Congregational Minister, H Stowell, who had been a War Chaplain. The collection was taken for the Church Army and the YMCA – the latter in particular having played such a fine role in supporting the troops throughout the conflict. And finally the Mayor sent a congratulatory telegraph to the King.

On Sunday 17 November Thanksgiving Services were held at Ennerdale, Irton, Drigg, Bigrigg, all the Millom Churches, Bootle, Hawkshead, Egton, Whicham, Hensingham (St John's and Methodist), Parton Congregational, Frizington, Egremont, St Bees, Cleator and many other churches.

On Tuesday 19 November a public celebration was held in Whitehaven to mark the conclusion of the Armistice. The children had been due to start back to school on this day; instead they suddenly found themselves in this celebration. With several bands, the procession made its way round town to St Nicholas' gates where the whole Corporation and other dignitaries had assembled. The children all marched past the platform where the Corporation were sitting carrying flags and banners and 'made a gay show'. A Belgian contingent also played a fine part in this celebration. 'Never was there such a procession for the numbers or the time it took to pass'.

The Mayor then gave an address, all were served tea in their schools, and the Mayor visited each school during the afternoon.

The children did not return to school until Monday 25 November because all schools were closed in the county due to the influenza outbreak, as a precaution. From the minutes of the Special Meeting of the Finance Committee of the Town Council on 20 December 1918 we know that £107 10/- was spent entertaining the children on the occasion of the Armistice Celebrations.

Yet the day was not one of rejoicing for all – in the same edition of the *Whitehaven News* there are several reports of the deaths of local soldiers.

'There were many homes in which there were quiet thankful hearts that beat as loyally as those of any of the flagwavers but in which the suddenly reinforced memory of the loss of their loved ones put joyous demonstration out of question.'

On the page before the ecstatic reports of the celebrations, the death in action of Edward Watson of Hensingham was announced. Directly below the reports of the celebrations, the death of Signaller Sydney Jackson Davis in action on 9 October was announced.

Such deaths were to continue for some time to come yet. The latest known death of a Whitehaven man from the effects of this war was on 10 September 1934, of CSM John Fletcher DCM, who died from the effects of having been shot in the stomach by a machine gun in March 1918.

And this is only Armistice yet, this is not a lasting peace.

After the signing of the formal Peace Treaty in 1919 the Government decreed that 19 July 1919 was to be the National Day of Celebration. For the Peace Celebrations a special committee was set up (Minute 33 of General Purposes Committee 30/4/1919) with a budget of £1,200, revised down on 6 May to 2d in the pound of the rates. This met on 19 May, 4 and 16 July and 5 August. A Subscription fund was to be set up to meet costs over and above the budget, although it appears that this did not in fact occur. The Earl of Lonsdale provided the Castle Grounds for the occasion. There were four sub-committees – Catering; Sports (Men); Sports (Children); and Procession, Parade and Carnival.

The initial programme was to be:
1) Procession of Sailors and Soldiers who had served, with various Women's Auxiliary Corps and Nurses
2) Dinner & Sports for Sailors and Soldiers
3) Entertainment of Women's Auxiliary Corps
4) Cycle and Motor Car Parade and Carnival
5) Regatta and Aquatic Sports
6) Tea & Sports for School Children & Souvenir to each child
7) Entertain Old Age Pensioners
8) Fireworks

When the date was in due course announced this was revised to: Entertain Soldiers and Sailors (Dinner & Sports); Entertain Widows and Parents of the Deceased (Tea); and Entertain School Children (Tea and Sports).

The final cost was Dinner £330 11/6d; Widows/Dependants Tea £30 0/6d; Soldiers and Sailors Sports £121 9/1d; Children's Tea £170 18/11d; Children's Sports £114 7/1d; Souvenirs (Peace Medals) £71 17/6d.

On the day at 10am, 1,200 Ex-Service men mustered at the Grand Hotel for a march through the town led by the Borough Band to the Cricket Field for a sports and bowling tournament. Lunch was at 12 noon in the Drill Sheds (voluntarily provided by The Globe Hotel, The Albion Hotel and the Cocoa Rooms), followed by more sports and bowling, and an evening al fresco dance led by the Borough Band.

At 5pm there was a Tea for the widows and parents of the fallen (over 250 in number) at the St Nicholas Parish Rooms presided over by the Mayoress

At 2.15pm, school children assembled at the market place, marched through the town (accompanied by the Borough Band, the Catholic Band and the Discharged Soldier's and Sailor's Band), saluting the flag at the town hall, and then adjourned to their schools for tea followed by sports at the Castle Grounds for the St James Infant and Junior Schools; at the Colliery Recreation Ground for St Beghs; St Gregory's and St Patricks and the Earl of Lonsdale Schools; and at the Cricket Field for the Council, Trinity and Crosthwaite Schools. Colonel Jackson also provided sweets for the Crosthwaite School pupils.

At 11 pm, tar barrels were lit for the national lighting of bonfires.

During the afternoon the Mayor visited the Infirmary for special food and entertainment (dinner and tea) and a concert. Four wounded soldiers were each given 5/- from the Government and 5/- each and cigarettes from the Mayor. At the workhouse, all 136 inmates were given special food at breakfast, dinner and tea. Dinner was roast beef and mutton with potatoes, followed by plum pudding.

The children's souvenirs were medals (Carlisle was the only other place in Cumberland to issue such medals). They were made by Mappin and Webb (Jewellers) out of an aluminium alloy. One (which is in private hands) was exhibited at the 2015 Beacon Exhibition.

At Hensingham the children paraded from the School to the Square at noon, followed by a service at St John's Church then a tea for all at a field lent by Noble Birkett, followed by sports and dancing.

At Moresby Parks the children held a parade led by the Colliery Band followed by tea for 250 children, sixty old people and widows and forty-five soldiers and then sports.

Similar events were held at Harrington (spread over four days); at Arlecdon/Frizington; Moor Row; Egremont; Seascale, and The Green (near Millom).

At Silecroft there was a tea (for over 300 people), free to all residents and visitors alike, with a procession to the shore and back followed by sports at Mrs Dixon's field, Hodgson Green, then fireworks and a bonfire at Arrad Hill. There were only three fights during the day!!

There were other celebrations reported in the *Whitehaven News* at Millom, Allithwaite, Seathwaite, Greenodd, Sawrey, Grasmere, Aspatria, Coniston, Gosforth, Ponsonby, Bootle, Ambleside, Hawkshead, High

Wray, Broughton, Askam, Netherwasdale, St Bees, Cleator Moor, Lamplugh, Drigg, Irton, Eskdale, Corney, Haile, Braystones, Beckermet, Maryport, Flimby and Lowick, and there were doubtless many other events in settlements large and small across the two counties of Cumberland and Westmorland.

In Wasdale there was a great bonfire on top of Buckbarrow Pike (viewed from Kidbeck How). Other bonfires were lit on Scafell Pike, Boonwood and Black Combe. On Scafell Pike 93 people inscribed their names in a book.

At Workington over 11,000 people attended a Thanksgiving Service in Lonsdale Park. This had been preceded by a march through town of over 1,000 ex-soldiers and sailors. The service ended with a gun salute, the Last Post and the National Anthem. This was followed by tea for all the schoolchildren and all the ex-servicemen (the latter at the New South Watts Street canteen). There were evening children's sports and dancing for all.

At Drigg all who served were at a later date presented with a silver cup by the Parish Council as a token of gratitude for their service, their suffering and, for some, their ultimate sacrifice. One, at least, of these survives – to John Edward Postlethwaite Coward. It was on display from January to March 2015 at the Beacon Museum, Whitehaven during their First World War exhibition. Both the village war memorial and the cup state that he was in the Border Regiment, but in fact he was in the Highland Light Infantry. From the Council Accounts Book (YSPC 16/3 at Whitehaven Record Office) we know that the Peace Celebrations as a whole cost the council £30 exactly. This was a large sum for a council with annual receipts of around £15 and annual expenditure of around £7 which was covered by reserves. Unfortunately we have no better breakdown of this cost (so we don't know how many cups were made) as the Minute Book of the council was withdrawn from the Archives by the Council in 1995.

But just 20 years later the world found itself at war. And one of many reasons for this is in Minute 2609 of Whitehaven Town Council meeting of 11 December 1918 – a minute which reflected a national mood, which was to become reality – namely that Germany repay the full costs incurred by the Allies of the war (and that the ex-Kaiser be handed over for trial) – these Reparations had a knock-on effect in terms of European politics and led directly to the rise of Adolf Hitler and the Nazi Party. And in 1939, war came again to Whitehaven.

Appendix

Border Regiment during WWI, actions and movements

1st Battalion

4 August 1914: Stationed at Maymyo, Burma at the outbreak of war.

9 December 1914: Embarked for England from Bombay landing at Avonmouth.

10 January 1915: Moved to Rugby to join the 87th Brigade of the29th Division.

17 March 1915: Mobilised for war and embarked for Gallipoli from Avonmouth via Alexandria and Mudros.

25 April 1915: Landed at Gallipoli and engaged in various actions against the Turkish Army.

9 January 1916: Evacuated to Mudros due to heavy casualties from combat, disease and severe weather, and then moved to Alexandria.

March 1916: Moved to France and engaged in various actions on the Western Front including;

During 1916: Albert; Transloy Ridges.

During 1917: First, Second and Third Scarpe; Langemarck; Broodseinde; Poelcapelle; Cambrai.

During 1918: Estaires; Messines; Hazebrouck; Bailleul; Outtersteene Ridge; Ploegsteert and Hill 63; Ypres; Courtrai.

11 November 1918: Ended the war in Belgium near Celles S.W. of Renaix.

Border Regiment pin cushion made by Private William Atkinson, 2nd Border, while convalescing in York Hospital in 1916. He was wounded at the Battle of Festubert.
(Royal War Records)

2nd Battalion

4 August 1914: Stationed at Pembroke Dock and then moved to Lyndhurst to join the 20th Brigade of the 7th Division.

6 October 1914: Mobilised for war and landed at Zeebrugge and engaged in various actions on the Western Front including;

During 1914: First Ypres.

December 1914: This Battalion took part in the Christmas Truce.

During 1915: Neuve Chapelle; Aubers; Festubert; Givenchy; Loos.
During 1916: Albert; Bazentin; High Wood; Delville Wood;
Guillemont; the Ancre.
During 1917: The German retreat to the Hindenburg Line; Arras;
Polygon Wood; Broodseinde; Poelcapelle; Second Passchendaele,
November 1917: Moved to Italy to strengthen the Italian resistance.
4 November 1918: Ended the war in Italy, Pozzo east of Pordenone.

3rd (Reserve) Battalion
4 August 1914: Stationed at Carlisle then moved to Shoeburyness.
January 1916: Moved to Conway and then Barrow.
March 1917: Moved to Great Crosby, near Liverpool until the end of
the war.

1/4th (Cumberland & Westmorland) Battalion Territorial Force
4 August 1914: Stationed at Carlisle and attached to the East Lancs.
Division and then moved to Barrow.
September 1914: Moved to Sittingbourne and transferred to the
Middlesex Brigade of the Home Counties Division.
29 October 1914: Embarked for India from Southampton arriving at
Rangoon December 1914: Division then broken up and remained in
India throughout the war.

1/5th (Cumberland) Battalion Territorial Force
4 August 1914: Stationed at Workington attached to the East Lancs.
Division and then moved to Barrow.
26 October 1914: Mobilised for war and landed at Le Havre to defend
the Lines of Communication.
5 May 1915: Transferred to 149th Brigade of the 50th Division.
20 December 1915: Transferred to 151st Brigade of the 50th Division
and continued to engage in various actions on the Western Front
including;
During 1915: St Julien; Frezenburg Ridge; Bellewaarde Ridge.
During 1916: Flers-Courcelette; Morval; Transloy Ridges.
During 1917: First Scarpe; Wancourt Ridge; Second Scarpe; Second
Passchendaele.
12 February 1918: Transferred as a Pioneer Battalion to the 66th Division.
During 1918: St Quentin; the Somme Crossings; Rosieres.
7 May 1918: Absorbed the personnel of 11th Battalion and transferred
to 97th Brigade of the 32nd Division

31 July 1918: Absorbed the cadre of the 11th Battalion and continued to engage in various actions on the Western Front including: Cambrai; the Selle.

11 November 1918: Ended the war in France, near Avesnes.

2/4th (Cumberland & Westmorland) Battalion Territorial Force

October 1914: Formed at Kendal and then moved to Blackpool.

4 March 1915: Embarked for India from Avonmouth arriving at Bombay 31 March 1915 and remained for the duration of the war.

2/5th (Cumberland) Battalion Territorial Force

October 1914: Formed at Kendal.

November 1915: Moved to Falkirk and joined the 2/4th and 2/5th of the Royal Scots Fusiliers to form the 13th Battalion of the 194th Brigade of the 65th Division.

January 1916: Absorbed by the 2/4th Royal Scots Fusiliers.

3/4th and 3/5th Battalion Territorial Force

March 1915: Formed and then moved to Ramsey, Isle of Man.

8 April 1916: Became the 4th and 5th (Reserve) Battalion.

1 September 1916: The 4th absorbed the 5th as part of the East Lancs. Reserve Brigade.

January 1917: Moved to Ripon and then Scarborough, finally to Filey where it remained.

6th (Service) Battalion

August 1914: Formed at Carlisle as part of the First New Army and then moved to Grantham to join the 33rd Brigade of the 11th Division and then moved to Frensham.

1 July 1915: Mobilised for war and embarked for Gallipoli from Liverpool via Mudros.

20 July 1915: Landed at Cape Helles.

31 July 1915: Moved back to Mudros.

7 August 1915: Landed at Suvla Bay.

18 December 1915: Evacuated to Imbros due to heavy losses from combat, disease and severe weather.

1 February 1916: Moved to Alexandria to defend the Suez Canal.

30 June 1916: Embarked for France from Alexandria landing at Marseilles and engaged in various actions on the Western Front including: Wundt-Werk; Flers-Courcelette; Thiepval.

During 1917: the Ancre; Messines; Langemarck; Polygon Wood; Broodseinde; Poelcapelle.

9 February 1918: Disbanded in France at Mazingarbe.

7th (Service) Battalion

7 September 1914: Formed at Carlisle as part of the Second New Army and then moved to Wool to join the 51st Brigade of the 17th Division and then moved to Andover.

January 1915: Moved to Bovington and then Winchester.

15 July 1915: Mobilised for war and landed at Boulogne and engaged in various actions on the Western Front including;

During 1916: Albert; Delville Wood.

During 1917: First and Second Scarpe; Roeux; First and Second Passchendaele.

22 September 1917: Absorbed twenty-one officers & 239 men of the now dismounted Westmorland & Cumberland Yeomanry, and became the 7th (Westmorland & Cumberland Yeomanry) Battalion.

During 1918: St Quentin; Bapaume; Amiens; Albert; Havrincourt; Epehy; Cambrai; the Selle; the Sambre.

11 November 1918: Ended the war in Aulnove, France.

8th (Service) Battalion

September 1914: Formed at Carlisle as part of the Third New Army then moved to Codford to join the 75th Brigade of the 25th Division, then to Boscombe.

May 1915: Moved to Romsey and then Aldershot.

27 September 1915: Mobilised for war and landed at Boulogne and engaged in various actions on the Western Front including;

During 1916: Vimy Ridge; Albert; Bazentin; Pozieres; Ancre Heights.

During 1917: Messines; Pilkem.

During 1918: St Quentin; Bapaume; Estaires; Messines; Bailleul; First and Second Kemmel.

22 June 1918: Transferred to the Composite Brigade of the 50th Division.

7 July 1918: Disbanded in France.

9th (Service) Battalion (Pioneer)

September 1914: Formed at Carlisle as part of the Third New Army and then moved to Lewes and Seaford to join the 66th Brigade of the 22nd Division and then moved to Eastbourne.

February 1915: Became a Pioneer Battalion of the 22nd Division, then moved to Seaford, on to Aldershot.

4 September 1915: Mobilised for war and landed at Havre.

29 October 1915: Embarked for Salonika from Marseilles and engaged in various actions against the Bulgarian Army including;

During 1916: Horseshoe Hill; Machukovo.

During 1917 and 1918: Doiran.

30 September 1918: Ended the war in Macedonia, N.W. of Lake Doiran.

10th (Reserve) Battalion

October 1914: Formed as a service battalion at Southend as part of the Fourth New Army

10 April 1915: Became a 2nd Reserve Battalion and then moved to Billericay.

September 1915: Moved to Seaford as part of the 4th Reserve Brigade.

1 September 1916: Absorbed into the Training Reserve Battalion.

11th (Service) Battalion (Lonsdale)

17 September 1914: Formed at Carlisle by the Earl of Lonsdale and an Executive Committee, then moved to Kendal and Workington.

October 1914: Moved to Blackhall Racecourse, Carlisle and then on to Prees Heath to join the 97th Brigade of the 32nd Division.

June 1915: Moved to Wensley and then Fovant, Salisbury Plain.

27 August 1915: Taken over by the War Office.

23 November 1915: Mobilised for war and landed at Boulogne and engaged in various actions on the Western Front including;

During 1916: Albert; Bazentin; the Ancre.

During 1917: the Ancre and the pursuit of the German army to the Hindenburg Line.

During 1918: First Arras; Amiens; Albert; Bapaume.

10 May 1918: Reduced to training cadre with surplus personnel transferred to the 1/5th Battalion.

13 May 1918: Transferred to the 66th Division.

31 July 1918: Cadre absorbed by the 1/5th Battalion.

12th (Reserve) Battalion

Formed from the depot companies of the 11th Battalion at Prees Heath as a local reserve battalion in the 17th Reserve Brigade.

1 September 1916: Absorbed into the 75th Training Reserve Battalion.

Sources

100 Years of St Bees, Douglas Sim (St Bees Parish Council, 1995)

Being Prepared, 100 years of scouting in Cumbria, Roy McNamara, Bookcase (2007)

Borough of Whitehaven Roll of Honour European War 1914-1918

Bulmer's History & Directory of Cumberland, 1901

Bygone Whitehaven, Volume Six, by Michael and Sylvia Moon, 1986

Caldbeck Characters (Caldbeck & District Local History Society, 1995)

Christmas Truce, Malcolm Brown (Leo Cooper, 1984)

Comrades in Conscience, Cyril Pearce (Francis Boutle, 2001)

Cumberland Iron, the Story of Hodbarrow Mine 1855-1968, A Harris (D Bradford Barton, 1970)

The Cumberland Coast, Neil Curry (Bookcase, 2007)

Cumbria, Within Living Memory, Cumbria Federation of Women's Insistutes, 1994

The Cumbria Village Book, WI (1991, Countryside Books)

Cumbrian Women Remembered, June Thistlethwaite (Ellenbank Press, 1995)

Discovering Egremont, EA Read (Titus Wilson & Son, Kendal, 1995)

Harrington Through the Years, Book 6, Harrington History Group

The Home Front in the Great War, David Bilton (Leo Cooper, 2003)

The Home Front, Peter Cooksley (Tempus, 2006)

The Irish in the Somme, Steven Moore (Local Press, Belfast, 2005)

The Lonsdale Battalion 1914-18, Colin Bardgett (Cromwell Press, 1993)

Millom Remembered, Bill Myers (Tempus, 2004)

Papers of Lieutenant-Colonel DJ Mason of Workington (edited by Thomas Thompson)

Railwaymen of Cumbria Remembered, Cumbria Railways Association. Researched and compiled by Peter Robinson, 2008

Ravenglass Through the Ages, Barbara Newton (BNFL, 1989)

Road Transport in Cumbria in the 19th Century, LA Williams (George Allen and Unwin, 1975)

Transport in Barrow in Furness, Harry Postlethwaite (Venture Publications, 2013)

Seascale, The Village of Seascale, the history and its people, Neville Ramsden (Copeland Research, 1998)

The Solway Firth, Brian Blake (the Regional Books Series, 1963)

Ulster and the Great War, Linen Hall Library, 10 September 2014, Jonathan Bardon

VCs of the First World War, Gerald Gliddon
The War Work of Auxiliary Hospitals and Voluntary Aid Detachments of Cumberland, Westmoreland and Part of North West Lancashire by George Hermon Griffin
Whitehaven: Its Streets, Its Principal Houses and Their Inhabitants, William Jackson 1878
Whitehaven and the Tobacco Trade, Nancy Eaglesham (Friends of Whitehaven Museum, 1979)

Online
www.airfieldinformationexhange.org (lists WWI places of Internment/PoW camps)
www.egremont2day.com/2014/03/remembering-the-great-wars-heroes
www.findagrave.com
Great War Forum, 1914-1918. **www.invisionzone.com**
Imperial War Museum, **www.iwm.org.uk**
www.ravenglass-railway.co.uk
www.stbees.org.uk
War Memorials Online, **www.warmemorials.org**
The Worcestershire Regimental Archives, The Worcestershire Regiment Museum.

Archives and Museums
Imperial War Museum, London
Beacon, Whitehaven
Rum Museum, Whitehaven
British Library, London
The National Archives, Kew, west London

Index